How to Read Descartes's *Meditations*

Other Titles of Interest from St. Augustine's Press

How to Read
Descartes's *Meditations*

Zbigniew Janowski

St. Augustine's Press
South Bend, Indiana

Manufactured in the United States of America.

1 2 3 4 5 6   24 23 22 21 20 19

Library of Congress Cataloging in Publication Data
Janowski, Zbigniew.
How to read Descartes's Meditations / Zbigniew Janowski. – 1st ed.
p. cm.
Includes bibliographical references and index.
ISBN 1-58731-355-3 (clothbound: alk. paper)
1. Descartes, René, 1596–1650. Meditationes de prima
philosophia. 2. First philosophy – History. I. Title.
B1854.J36 2005
194 – dc22   2005029166

ST. AUGUSTINE'S PRESS
www.staugustine.net

To Jean-Luc Marion
Richard (Red) Watson
and in memory of a dear friend and teacher
Leszek Kolakowski

Contents

Foreword

This collection of articles is neither a systematic exposition of the *Meditations* nor is it a collection of studies of each Meditation. Rather, it is a collection of "insights" into Descartes's *Meditations*. Each chapter deals with a fairly narrow point of Descartes's philosophy that has not been given an elaborate account in Cartesian scholarship nor has been sufficiently explored.

My focus is primarily the influence of past thinkers on Descartes: Aristotle, St. Thomas (Meditations II and VI), Duns Scotus (Meditation III), St. Augustine (Meditation IV), and Descartes's use of some of the ecclesiastical documents (Letter to the Sorbonne).

The name of Aristotle pops up throughout Descartes's letters. However, it is not always clear whether Descartes has in mind the ancient philosopher or his medieval interpreters, particularly St. Thomas. Descartes knew Aristotle's writings first-hand. But which ones in particular did he read or positioned himself against while writing the *Meditations*? One could assume, as I did in writing chapter III, that he read *De anima*. However, *De anima* is only one among many works which form a long chain of considerations that explain the Aristotelian theory of the soul, cognition, and the movement of animals, including man. Many of Aristotle's writings – e.g., *De motu animalium, parva naturalia, De generatione animalium*, etc. – are hardly of interest to anyone but Aristotle scholars, and only seldom are they read by Cartesian scholars. To properly understand Aristotle's theory of movement, and thus Descartes's alternative explanation, one needs to go beyond *De anima*.

While I was writing the chapter on the Second and Sixth Meditations, in which I try to read Descartes against Aristotle, I realized the vastness of the topic. An analysis that does justice to Aristotle's or Aquinas's cannot be comprised within the confines of a single chapter. This chapter, I hope, provides valuable hints and will make others devote their scholarly energy to a full-length study of the relationship between Aristotle, St. Thomas and Descartes.[1]

Other chapters in this collection deal with St. Augustine and Duns Scotus. As I showed in my *Augustinian-Cartesian Index* and *Cartesian Theodicy*, St. Augustine's influence can be felt throughout the *Meditations*. Here, however, I wanted merely to point out the role which the Augustinian theology played in the notoriously difficult-to-understand Cartesian metaphysics in Meditation IV. In the chapter on Meditation III, I explore the possible influence of Duns Scotus on Descartes.

In contradistinction to Meditations II, III, IV, and VI, Meditation I is relatively free from an obvious influence of a single thinker. My concern in the chapter on Meditation I is the implicit presence of the Doctrine of the Eternal Truths. However, once again, this does not mean that one could not point out to someone's influence on Descartes in Meditation I. The most suitable candidate, in my opinion, is Francis Bacon. His impact, which I briefly presented earlier in my *Augustinian-Cartesian Index*, does not limit itself to textual affinities. It may come as something of a shock to suggest that of all the items in Descartes's armory the least Cartesian of all is what is Cartesian *par excellence*: the method of doubt. Doubt as the starting point of philosophy is prominent in Francis Bacon under the term "Idols." It is enough to juxtapose Bacon's *Advancement of Learning* and Descartes's *Meditations* to notice that what Bacon calls "Idols" Descartes calls "preconceived opinions." Like the "Idols" in Bacon, the "preconceived opinions" in Descartes cloud one's mind.

However, there is more to textual influences. Unlike Descartes,

---

1   Besides Jean-Luc Marion's *Sur l'ontologie grise de Descartes* (*Descartes's Grey Ontology*, translated by Sarah E. Donahue (South Bend, Ind.: St. Augustine's Press, 2019), which analyzes Aristotle's impact on the early Descartes, such a book has not been written.

who was a philosopher working within the Catholic tradition, and very aware of his theological "commitments," Bacon was a Protestant. The general idea underlying the Great Reformation was the rejection of Tradition and, consequently, much of the Catholic dogma. Thus what was initially an approach in Protestant theology – to purify the faith of all its dogmatic, "Catholic," ornaments – took on the form of a method in the philosophy of the Protestant Bacon, and via Bacon to Descartes. In other words, the core of Descartes's "Catholic" philosophy sprang, paradoxically, from the seeds planted by the Protestant Reformation.[2]

I would extend my warm thanks to several friends and colleagues who read different parts of this book: Jean-Luc Marion, Leszek Kolakowski, Vincent Carraud, Tad Schmaltz, Emanuela Scribano, Olivier Dubouclez, and François Azouvi. I would also like to thank the Earhart Foundation and Mr. Tony Sullivan for the generous grant that made the work on this book possible.

---

2 The same goes for the notion of "subjectivity," which can be traced to Luther's division between "inner" and "outer" man – a distinction he draws on the first few pages of his *The Freedom of the Christian*. This fact was already noticed by Feuerbach. See also the general treatment of this topic by Leszek Kolakowski, "The Philosophical Role of the Reformation: Martin Luther and the Origins of Subjectivity," in *The Two Eyes of Spinoza and Other Essays on Philosophers* (South Bend, Ind.: St. Augustine's Press, 2004).

How to Read Descartes's Letter to the Sorbonne: Is Descartes's Conception of the Soul Orthodox?[1]

"I have always thought," Descartes writes at the very outset of his Letter to the Faculty of Theology at the Sorbonne, "that two topics – namely God and the Soul – are prime examples of subjects where demonstrative proofs ought to be given with the aid of philosophy rather than theology."[2] And in the next paragraph, he adds:

> As regards the soul, many people have considered that it is not easy to discover its nature, and some have even had the audacity to assert that, as far as human reason goes, there are persuasive grounds for holding that the soul dies along with the body and that the opposite view is based on faith alone. But in its 8th session the Lateran Council held under Leo X condemned those who take this position, and establish the truth; so I have not hesitated to attempt this task as well.[3]

1 Originally published in *Revue de Métaphysique et de Morale*, No. 1, 2000. Reprinted with revisions. All citations from Descartes's works are from Charles Adam and Paul Tannery (eds.), *Oeuvres de Descartes*, 2nd edition, 11 vols. (Paris: Vrin, 1974–1986). This is abbreviated to AT. Citations in English from Descartes's works are from J. Cottingham, R. Stoothoff, D. Mardoch, and A. Kenny (eds.), *The Philosophical Writings of Descartes*, 3 vols. (Cambridge: Cambridge University Press, 1984–1995). This is abbreviated to CSM, with the exception of vol. III, which is abbreviated to CSMK.

2 AT VII, 1; CSM II, 3.

3 AT VII, 3; CSM II, 4.

Like St. Thomas in the Preface to the *Summa Contra Gentiles*,[4] Descartes presents his *Meditations* as a piece of Christian apologetics. It is addressed to, and directed against, unbelievers, who, in order to "lay down the spirit of contradiction," need to be persuaded by philosophical arguments that God exists and the soul does not die with the body.[5] Besides this purely apologetic objective, Descartes's goals are to vanquish skepticism, to build new foundations for the sciences, and to establish the "foundation of all human certitude."[6] Of all Descartes's objectives, only the attempt

4   By making a reference to St. Thomas's *Summa Contra Gentiles* I do not merely mean to draw conceptual similarities. Descartes knew *this* work by St. Thomas (see my *Augustinian-Cartesian Index*, pp. 168–73). There is good reason to think that in thinking of the structural arrangement of his opus, he had St. Thomas in mind. Also, insofar as St. Thomas's system is the most complete synthesis of Christian philosophy, *Summa Philosophiae Christianae*, Descartes's *Meditations*, with its pretensions to replace Scholastic philosophy, can be said to be the *summa philosophiae modernae*. If this is the case, one can wonder in what sense Descartes thought his philosophy could better satisfy the demands of Christian philosophy than that of St. Thomas. St. Thomas's *Summa* addresses four points which are, respectively, subjects of the four parts of this work: God, man, providence (i.e., the relationship between God and man), and salvation. It leaves no questions unanswered. If one contrasts Descartes's "summa" with that of St. Thomas, Descartes's considerations overlap only with the first two parts of the *Summa*: God and man. Descartes does not deal with the question of either providence or salvation; nor could he, for his conception of God seems to preclude such knowledge.

       What remains problematic is, of course, Descartes's attempt to present his *Meditations* as a piece of Christian apologetics on the one hand, and as an anti-Aristotelian work on the other. There is no reason to think that the apologetic character of Descartes's work is a smokescreen for his allegedly secular intentions. For example, Francis Bacon, whose philosophy inscribes itself in the Cartesian project of the Mastery of Nature, does not appear to be concerned with presenting his philosophy as a piece of Christian apologetics.

5   St. Thomas, SCG, I, 2 [3].

6   In the first paragraph of the First Meditation Descartes writes: "I realized that it was necessary, once in the course of my life, to demolish everything completely and start again right from the foundations if I wanted to establish anything at all in the sciences that was stable and likely to last" (AT VII, 17; CSM II, 17). Clearly, the objective in the Letter to the Sorbonne and the objective in the First Meditation seem to diverge: one is religious and apologetic; the other is of an epistemological nature.

to demonstrate the immortality of the soul is supported by the decree of the Fifth Lateran Council (1512–1517) cited in his Letter to the Sorbonne.

The bull Descartes invokes is the *Apostolici Regiminis* (19 December 1513).

> Since in our days (and we painfully bring this up) the sower of cockle, ancient enemy of the human race, has dared to disseminate and advance in the field of the Lord a number of pernicious errors always rejected by the faithful, especially concerning the nature of the rational soul, namely, that it is mortal, or one in all men, and some rashly philosophizing affirmed that this is true at least according to philosophy, in our desire to offer suitable remedies against a plague of this kind, with the approval of this holy Council, we condemn and reject all who assert that [1] the intellectual soul is mortal, or [2] is one in all men, and those who cast doubt on these truths, since it [the soul] is not only truly in itself and essentially the form of the human body [*forma corporis*], as was defined in the canon of Pope CLEMENT V our predecessor of happy memory published in the (general) Council of VIENNE but it is also multiple according to the multitude of bodies into which it is infused, multiplied, and to be multiplied. . . . And since [3] truth never contradicts truth, we declare every assertion contrary to the truth of illumined faith to be altogether false; and, that it may not be permitted to dogmatize otherwise, we strictly forbid it, and we declare that all who adhere to errors of this kind are to be shunned and to be punished as detestable and abominable infidels who disseminate most damnable heresies and who weaken the Catholic faith.[7]

7   The Latin text reads: "Cum . . . zizaniae seminator . . . nonnullos perniciosisimos errors, a fidelibus semper explosos, in argo Domini superseminare et augere sit ausus, de natura praesertim animae rationalis, quod videlicet mortalis sit, aut unica in cunctis hominibus, et nonnulli temere philosophantes, secundum saltem philosophiam verum id esse asseverent: contra huiusmodi pestem opportune remedia adhibere cupientes, hoc sacro approbante Concilio damnamus et reprobamus omnes asserentes, animam intellectivam mortalem esse, aut unicam in cunctis hominibus, et haec in dubium verentes, cum illa non solum vere per se et essentialiter humani corporis forma existat, sicut in canone felicis recor-

The objects of condemnation were the "pernicious errors" of the Neo-Aristotelians, who maintained that the soul is mortal, and the errors of the Averroists, according to whom the soul is one in all men. The third point ([3]) condemns the so-called "double truth" doctrine of the Catholic Averroists at the University of Paris, who propounded to believe as theologians what they denied as philosophers.

When the Church condemned the heresies, their influence was so widespread, especially in Italy, that as Antonio Ricobboni remarked, "almost all Italy was converted to the error [of the Averroists]."[8] In the first quarter of the sixteenth century the situation reached the point that one "no longer [passed] for a man of cultivation, unless one put forth heterodox opinions regarding the Christian faith."[9] Pietro Pomponazzi, against whom, among others, the Bull was directed, openly declared that, "if the lawgiver declared the soul immortal, he had done so without troubling himself about the truth."[10] Oddly enough, to put an end to the

dationis Clementis papae V praedecessoris Nostri in [generali] Viennensi Concilio edito continetur, verum et immortalis et pro corporum quibus infunditur multitudine singulariter multiplicabilis , et multiplicata, et multiplicanda sit . . ." *Enchiridion Symbolorum, Definitionum et Declarationum De Rebus Fidei Et Morum*, ed. by Henricus Denzinger, #738.

   For details concerning the condemnation, see Ernest Renan, *Averroes et l'averroïsme* (Paris, 1861), pp. 362–67; and J. Roger Charbonnel, *La pensée italienne au XVI siècle et le courant libertain* (Paris, 1919), p. 229.

8   Antoni Riccoboni, *De gymnasio patavino* (Padua, 1598), VI, chapter x, fol. 134. Quoted from *The Renaissance Philosophy of Man*, ed. by E. Cassirer, P.O. Kristeller, J. H. Randall (Chicago: The University of Chicago Press, 1948), p. 265, footnote 22.

9   Leopold Ranke, *The History of the Popes, Their Church and State* (London: Henry G. Bohn, 1853) vol. I, p. 56.

10   "Peter of Mantua has asserted that according to the principles of philosophy and the opinion of Aristotle, the reasoning soul is or appears to be mortal, contrary to the determination of the Lateran Council; the pope commands that the said Peter shall retract, otherwise that he be proceeded against" (*Petrus de Mantua assertuit quod anima rationalis secumdum propria philosophiae et mentem Aristotelis sit seu videatur mortalis, contra determinationem concilii Lateranensis; papa mandat ut dictus Petrus revocet; alias contra ipsum procedatur*) (13 June, 1518). *Ibid.*, vol. I, p. 55 (footnote).

controversy, the Pope requested the Averroist Nifo to launch an attack against Pomponazzi. It is not clear, however, why the Pope encouraged an Averroist, whose doctrine of the soul ("the soul is one in all men") was no less "pernicious" to the Christian faith than that of the Alexandrians, to take a stance against Pomponazzi. As a contemporary historian observed, Leo X, who "loved a good fight,"[11] made the opposing parties fight against each other. A different explanation was suggested by Emil Bréhier, according to whom, the Alexandrian doctrine was in the Pope's eyes even more dangerous than that of the Averroists.[12] The heresies did not disappear overnight after the condemnation, but started to decline, and the problem was more or less dead by the time of the Council of Trent (1545–1563). It was not even discussed during its sessions. The authors of *The Catechism of the Council of Trent* (1565) contented themselves with a short statement: "the soul is immortal" (article xi). The year 1619, the year of the trial of Cremonini, a professor at Padua, marks the end of Neo-Aristotelianism in Italy.[13] In France, the doctrine of the Alexandrians was never as influential as in Italy and ceased to be a problem for the Church even earlier.

The *Meditations* were published in 1641; that is, one hundred twenty eight years after the Bull had been issued and, as far as one can tell, not much of the old controversy was left from the times

11 "[The clergy in Venice] persuaded the Patriarch and the Doge to burn the book and proclaim him a heretic. A copy was sent to his patron, Cardinal Bembo, the Platonist, to be condemned in Rome. But Bembo found no heresy in it, and Leo X, who loved a good fight, encouraged both sides in the controversy" (Paul Oskar Kristeller, "Pietro Pomponazzi," in the *Renaissance Philosophy of Man*, pp. 274–75. The most exhaustive study of this question is Etienne Gilson's "Autour de Pomponazzi: Problématique de 'immortalité de l'âme en Italie au début du XVI siècle,' " *Archives d'histoire doctrinale et littéraire du Moyen Age* (1961), pp. 164–279.

12 Emil Bréhier, *Histoire de la Philosophie*, vol. I, part 3 (Paris: PUF, 1967 ed.), p. 673.

13 In Renan's view: "[C]e libertinage d'opinions qui donne une physionomie si originale au nord-est de l'Italie durant le XVIe siècle, disparaît avec le péripatétisme arabe dans la première moitie du XVIIe" (*op, cit.*, p. 415); "En 1628, Gabriel Naude trouve encore l'averroisme dominant a Padoue. Le mort de Cremonini (1631) peut être considéré comme la limite du règne de cette philosophie" (*ibid.*, p. 413).

when the Holy See condemned the "pernicious errors." Secondly, the Bull condemned three propositions: (1) "the soul is mortal," (2) "the soul is one in all men," and (3) "the truth of this assertion ([1] and [2]) holds good . . . in philosophy," i.e., "between faith and reason no true dissension can ever exist, since the same God, who reveals mysteries and infuses faith, has bestowed on the human soul the light of reason."[14] In the Letter to the Sorbonne, Descartes mentions only the first error (the soul is mortal); he does not even allude to the other two condemned propositions. This is rather a strange omission considering the fact that the Bull is very specific as to who the *non nulli qui* (some people) who disseminate the "pernicious errors" are. Was Descartes's omission due to a simple carelessness, or did he deliberately disregard the other two points? In other words, why did Descartes, who, as he never tired of repeating, had limited knowledge of theology, use the old Bull in the first place?

Given the problems Descartes envisaged in receiving approbation from the Sorbonne for the *Meditations*, one can assume that fear of opposition[15] made him devise an appropriate tactic, such as, for example, including in the Letter to the Sorbonne an important Church document which would give support to his enterprise. This is speculation only, but nonetheless it is not improbable. Although the papal decree was one hundred twenty eight years old, and most of its contents were irrelevant to the doctrinal problems in 1641, it contained one important point, which Descartes did not fail to point out in the Letter. The Bull explicitly gave the non-theologians license to inquire into the question of the nature of the human soul. At the very outset of the Letter, Descartes reminds the Sorbonne theologians that questions such as the immortality of the soul and the existence of God belong even more to the domain of philosophy than to theology (*Semper existimavi duas quaestiones, de Deo & de Anima, praecipuas esse exiis quae Philosophiae potius quam Theologiae ope sunt demonstrandae*). Next Descartes goes on to refresh the theologians' memory that it

14 The First Vatican Council, Session III, April 24, 1870. Denzinger, *op. cit.*, #1797.
15 Cf. letters to Mersenne, 31 March 1641 (AT III, 349–50; CSMK III, p. 177), and to Gibieuf, 11 November 1640 (AT III, 237; CSMK III, 157–58).

was the Holy Father himself who "expressly mandat[ed] the Christian philosophers that they should dissolve the arguments of [those who dared to say that the soul is mortal] and prove the truth according to their abilities."[16]

In 1641 the controversy against which the decree of the Lateran Council was directed and which it tried to counteract was dead or was at best a pale reflection of an old affair, and Descartes could not seriously believe that the Pope's call was still in effect. Given that the Letter was supposed to be read by the theologians, Descartes could not count on his readers' ignorance of the contents of the Bull – unless the Bull was forgotten even by the theologians. Nor could he believe in good faith that his readers would really think that the Pope's call on philosophers to oppose a doctrine that had been dead for at least several decades had any significance in his time. Nor, again, was he so naive to think that what Leo X really wanted to say was that the non-theologians should meddle with questions of faith and theology. Already at the time of the Lateran Council, Cajetan himself expressed concern about the Pope's decree, foreseeing the possibility that once philosophers are allowed to inquire into questions such as the immortality of the soul, they will not leave the articles of faith intact (*R. P. D. Nicolaus, episcopus Bergomensis, dixit quod non placebat sibi quodtheologi imponerent philosophis disputantibus de veritate (l. unitate) intellectus. . . . R. P. D. Thomas [Cajetan], generalis ord. praedicatorum, dixit quod non placet secunda pars bullae, praecipiens philosophis ut publice persuadendo doceant veritatem fidei*).[17]

16 The text of the Bull to which Descartes refers reads: "Insuper omnibus et singulis philosophis in universitatibus studiorum generalium, et alibi publice legentibus, districte praeciendo mandamus, ut cum philosophorum principia aut conclusions, in quibus a recta fide deviare noscuntur, auditoribus suis legerint, seu explanavierint, quale hoc de animae mortalitate aut unitate, et mundi aeternitate, ac alia huiusmodi, teneantur eisdem veritatem religionis christiane omni conatu manifestum facere, et persuadendo pro posse docere, ac omni studio huiusmodi philosophorum argumenta, cum omnia solubilia existant, pro viribus excludere atque resolvere."

17 *Sacrorum Conciliorum Nova et Amplissima Collectio . . .* vol. 2 (Paris, 1901), p. 843, left column. According to the great Austrian historian of

Descartes probably never thought his appeal would be given credence; however, as long as he pretended that he acted in good faith, he could always seek recourse to the Bull and point out the passage where the Pope commands the non-theologians to resolve the problem of the nature of the soul.[18] In other words, the decree of the Lateran Council seems to have provided Descartes with what he needed: an explicit call for non-theologians to establish the truth of the immortality of the soul. If one limited oneself to citing only carefully selected fragments from the Bull, or passing in silence over its other parts – as Descartes did – it might appear that the Lateran Council welcomed all proofs of the immortality of the soul as long as they asserted man's individual immortality. Out of context, or selectively cited, the Pope's decision might indeed seem to be what the fragment cited in the Letter to the Sorbonne says.

If we scrutinize the Bull carefully, there is, however, one point that Descartes either forgot to cite or, what is more probable, deliberately decided not to bring to the attention of the Sorbonne the-

the Papacy, Ludwig Pastor, "the Bull was a practical weapon against the inroads which a paganized humanism was making among the clergy, for the university professors were directed to give a foremost place to what is now called apologetic theology, and the priests who were desirous of following the humanist curriculum were enjoined to complete a five years' course of theology or canon law as the most effectual breakwater to oppose a false philosophy. Even in the council-hall itself the atmosphere of the new ideas seems to have made itself felt; thus the objection raised by the Bishop of Bergamo had a tinge of the condemned propositions. The general of the Dominicans, Cajetan, pleaded for freer treatment of philosophy, because, apparently, he dreaded an intermixture of this science with theology." *The History of the Popes from the Close of the Middle Ages*, vol. 8 (Consortium Books), p. 390.

18 When Cremonini was accused of teaching Aristotle in such a way that it did not conform to the teaching of the Catholic Church, he made a laughing stock of the inquisitor: "A la date du 3 juillet 1619, le grand inquisiteur de Padoue lui [Cremonini] écrit pour lui rappeler le décret du concile de Lateran, qui ordonne aux professeurs de réfuter sérieusement les erreurs qu'ils exposent, et il lui demande une rétraction . . ." To which Cremonini responded: "qu'il ne dépendait pas de lui changer ses écrits, lesquels avaient reçu l'approbation du sénat, et qu'étant paye pour expliquer Aristote, il se croirait oblige de rendre ses honoraires, s'il enseignait autre chose que ce qu'il croit être réellement la pensée d'Aristote." Renan, *op. cit.*, pp. 412–13.

ologians. Leo X reiterated Clement V's edict, *De Summa Trinitate et fide catholica* (6 May 1312):

> Furthermore, with the approval of the above mentioned sacred council [the Council of Vienne] we reprove as erroneous and inimical to the Catholic faith every doctrine or position rashly asserting or turning to doubt that the substance of the rational or intellective soul truly and in itself is not a form of the human body, defining, so that the truth of sincere faith may be known to all, and the approach to all errors may be cut off, lest they steal in upon us, that whoever shall obstinately presume in turn to assert, define, or hold that the rational or intellective soul is not the form of the human body in itself and essentially must be regarded as a heretic.[19]

Leo X repeated these words almost verbatim:

> For the soul not only truly exists of itself (*per se*) and essentially (*essentialitater*) as the form of the human body (*humani corporis forma*), as it is said in the canon of our predecessor of happy memory, pope Clement V, promulgated in the general council of Vienne, but is also immortal.

Both Councils asserted not only that the soul is immortal, and that all men have individual souls, but that the soul is the form of the human body. Thus in the light of Leo X's bull – that Descartes cites on the very first page of the *Meditations* with such confidence as supporting his enterprise – it was heretical not only to maintain the Neo-Aristotelian and Averroist doctrines, but also to advance a conception that would not accord with the Scholastic proposition *anima humani corporis forma*. To contradict the decree of the Councils of Vienne and Lateran was tantamount to spreading heresy.

I

The proposition *anima humani corporis forma* has not been created in the philosophico-theological vacuum. According to Aristotle, the human soul is the form of the body, the principle of its movement (*De anima*, I, 408–9), and a substance inseparable from its body (II, 412b10–413a5). The Scholastics revised

---

19 Denzinger, *op. cit.*, #481.

Aristotle's definition in one important respect. Aristotle said nothing about the immortality of the soul. *Anima* (Gr. *psyche*) or *forma* was to Aristotle the principle of organization of matter and the principle of the body's movement, and it was subject to death the same way the body was. To ensure the immortality of the soul St. Thomas conceived of the human soul not only as conferring the form on the body (i.e., act of being), but also as possessing substantiality. The soul for the Scholastics was not solely the organizing principle of matter and of the body's life, but could outlive the body. The body, in accordance with the definition of substance, is not a substance, but due to its union with the soul (form), it has substantiality. This substantial union between the soul and its body was, as the Scholastics called it, *harmonia* (Gr. *entelechy*). Accordingly, the Thomistic man is neither a soul nor is he his body – he is both. Besides, in his cognitive operations he needs a body – at least in the earthly life[20] – as much as he needs a soul.

When in 1312 the Pope Clement V accepted the proposition that the soul is *per se* or *essentialitater* the form of the body, the Church condemned the doctrine of John Peter Olivi, whose doctrine – the Thomists claimed – broke that essential unity of man. According to Olivi, the soul is composed of three parts: the vegetative form, the sensitive form, and the intellectual form; the higher form of the soul (intellectual) moves the lower forms: vegetative and sensitive. The soul's unity is guaranteed by the existence of the spiritual matter. Hence Olivi concludes, the intellectual part of the soul does not "inform" the body directly (*per se* or *essentialiter*). This meant that the soul, insofar as it is rational, is united substantially to body, but not formally. Olivi put forth his conception against the Thomists, who, in his eyes, compromised the Christian belief: "if the intellectual soul is the form of the body in the strong

20 "From all this we can conclude that the soul understands in three ways after death. In one, it understands through species which it received from things while it was in the body. In the second, through species which God infuses in it at the time of its separation from the body. In the third, by seeing separated substances and looking at the species of things which are in them. But this last mode does not lie within their free choice but within that of the separated substance . . ." St. Thomas, *Summa Theologica*, Ia, Q. 19, Art. 1, Reply, in *Truth*, translated by James V. McGlynn, s.j. (Chicago: Henry Regnery Company, 1953), vol. 2, p. 319.

Aristotelian sense of 'form,' then either the soul is mortal or the body is immortal."[21] As far as one can say, the condemnation of Olivi's doctrine was brought about by the followers of St. Thomas. Yet, Clement V's Bull was broad enough to make room for the Scotist doctrine, according to which, besides the principal substantial form which is the soul itself, the body has a secondary corporeal form (*forma corporeitatis*) – provided that they preserve the unity of matter and form.

The contrast between Descartes and the Scholastics is nowhere more visible than at the very heart of Descartes's method – the Universal Doubt. Given the substantial union that exists between the Thomistic man's soul and his body, had Descartes shared St. Thomas's conception of man, the whirlpool of Cartesian Doubt through which Descartes passed through his meditator, would "suck in" not only his body but also his soul. St. Thomas could not write, as Descartes does in the Second Meditation: "I am, then, in the strict sense only a thing that thinks; that is, I am a mind, or intelligence, or intellect, or reason."[22]

Descartes's words would be unintelligible to the Scholastics. If Descartes's meditator – since the term "man" can no longer be applied in this context – emerges victorious from this epistemologically and ontologically purifying procedure, it is only because the Cartesian soul is not the form of body the existence of which the Universal Doubt has just suspended. Therefore, the soul's union with the body is not substantial.

The *res cogitans* in the above-quoted passage from the Second Meditation is not a soul, but a mind (*mens*), or intelligence (*animus*), or intellect (*intellectus*), or reason (*ratio*). What is missing from the list is the Latin term *anima*, that is, soul. It would seem

21 Olivi II Sent., q. 50 (II, 77). Quoted after David Burr, "The Persecution of Peter Olivi," in *Transactions of the American Philosophical Society*, vol. 66 (1976), pt. 5, p. 53. See also an extensive study by Theodor Schneider, *Die Einheit Des Menschen: Die antropologische Formel "anima forma corporis" im sogenannten Korrektorienstreit und bei Petrus Johannis Olivi. Ein Beitrag zur Vorgeschichte des Konzils von Vienne* (Munster: Verlag Aschendorff, 1973), pp. 1311–12. *Sein Quellen und Sein Geschichte* (Munster: Verlag der Anchendorttschen Verlagsbuch-handlung, 1934), pp. 353–86.

22 AT VII, 18; CSM II, 19.

that the passage in the Second Meditation does not provide us with
any important insight into the union between the soul and the
body and the character of this union. Yet one might counter argue.
In Latin – especially in the Augustinian Latin[23] – *anima* designates
the animating principle of bodies. Both man, animals, and plants
have *anima*. The second term used by Descartes, *animus*, occasionally signifies *anima*, but its primary meaning is that of the
rational soul, found only in humans and angels.[24] A passage in *De
quantitate animae*, XII, 22, reads: "[*animus* is] a substance shar-
ing in reason and suited to the regulation of the body" ([*animus
est*] *substantia quaedam rationis particeps, regendo corpori
accommodata*); in *De Civitate Dei*, VII, 23, 1, *animus* is said to be
summus gradus animae. Sometimes St. Augustine identifies *animus* with *mens* (*De Civitate Dei*, XI,3).[25] Next, *ratio* (reason), fre-
quently equated by St. Augustine with *mens*, is called "the gaze of
the mind" (*aspectus mentis*).[26] In *De Civitate Dei*, XI, 3, *anima* is
identified with *mens*, like in the following sentence: "There are
matters other than sensory perceptions which are perceived by the
mind and the reason" (*itade his quae animo ac mente sentiur*). In
De magistro, XII, 40, in turn, St. Augustine states, as though antic-
ipating Descartes's demonstration of the *res cogitans* by eleven
hundred years: "But when we have to do with things which we
behold with the mind (*mente*), that is, with the intellect (*intellectu*) and with reason (*ratione*), we speak of things which we look
upon directly in the inner light of truth which illumines the inner

23 See Gilson, *The Christian Philosophy of St. Augustine* (New York:
    Random House, 1960), pp. 269–72; and Vernon J. Bourke, "The Body-
    Soul Relation in the Early Augustine," in *Collectanea Augustinana*,
    Joseph C. Schnaubelt, o.s.a., Frederick Van Fleteren, eds. (New York:
    Peter Lang, 1990), pp. 435–50.
24 In sermon CCXIV, St. Augustine states, "Thus all visible and invisible
    creatures, or some rational mind, can participate in unchangeable truths,
    known to an angel or to a man" (*Omnes ergo visibiles invisibilesque
    creaturas, vel quiquid rationibili mente potest esse particeps incom-
    mutabilis veritatis, sicuti angelus et homo*).
25 See also A. Gardeil, "Le 'MENS' d'après S. Augustine et S. Thomas D'
    Aquin," *Revue des sciences philosophiques et théologiques* (2 April
    1924), pp. 145–61.
26 *Soliloquia* I, vii, 13.

man and is inwardly enjoyed" (*Cum vero de iis agitur quae mente conspicimus, id est, intellectu atqueratione, ea quidem loquimur quae praesentia contuemur in illa interioreluce veritatis, qua ipse qui dicitur homo interior, illustratur et fruitur . . .*).

Each of the terms used by Descartes is more ample or inclusive than *anima*. Secondly, *anima* means first and foremost the principle of life of bodies, and was applied indiscriminately to both man and animals. Descartes's meditator, after he has gone through the whirlpool of doubt, is no longer a man of flesh and bones, and, therefore, does not need *anima*. The absence of *anima* from the *res cogitans* in the Second Meditation is, then, required by the Universal Doubt that suspended the existence of bodies.

II

Contrary to the impression Descartes tried to convey, his method of Doubt is not ontologically innocent: it presupposes the conception of the soul whose union with the body is of a more or less "accidental" nature. Descartes's meditator, in order to "survive" the whirlpool of Doubt, must have a soul that is not the Scholastic form of a body.

In her "Aquinas Lecture," Marjorie Grene argued very forcefully that, "substantial forms, like real qualities, are banished everywhere from nature, only not in the case of the human being. . . . We must take Descartes's teaching here quite seriously: there is in all the world only one substantial form, ours, but that one there undeniably is."[27] Tempting as her interpretation is, it is not entirely convincing. In the *Summa Contra Gentiles* I, 84, St. Thomas claims that God cannot create a man who would be an ass, since God cannot make contradictions true. To create a man who would be an ass would require combining the rational with the irrational. In other words, as ass's body requires an appropriate form, so the human body requires the human form. This is not the case for Descartes. According to the doctrine of the eternal truths, God can make contradictions true, and hence He can place a rational soul into an ass's body. The Cartesian doctrine of the eternal truths is

27 *Descartes among the Scholastics* (Milwaukee: Marquette University Press, 1991), p. 21. Emphasis mine.

irreconcilable with the substantial union between the soul and the body; in fact it destroys this union. In other words, once we accept the Cartesian doctrine of the eternal truths and the resulting conception of the soul as *res cogitans*, we inevitably must accept a corollary that there is nothing intrinsically necessary in my having my – human – body rather than that of an ass. In contrast to the *hylemorphism* of the Scholastics, the Cartesian soul's union with the body not only is very loose, but it seems that there is nothing in this union that could explain why I have any body at all.[28]

28 Cf. *Summa Contra Gentiles*, II, 57 (especially 2–3) where Thomas points out that Plato's "sailor in the ship" amounts to reducing man to a being by accident (*ens per accidens*).

29 The traditional way in which dogma in the Catholic Church has been formed is by condemnation of a doctrine considered as heretical. The condemnation of Olivi gave the Church occasion to accept the Thomistic (-Scotist) conception as Her own. This doctrine, as far as I am able to verify, has never been altered, and was reaffirmed again in the 19th century. In 1857, Pope Pius IX condemned the errors of Antoni Gunter, and the question of the soul's nature returned again: "We know that in the same books there is harm to the Catholic opinion and teaching concerning man, who is composed of body and soul, and that the rational soul may of itself be the true and immediate form of the body" (*Noscimus, iisdem libris laedi catholicam sententiam ac doctrinam de homine, qui corpore et anima ita absolvatur, ut anima eaque rationalis sit vera per se atque immediatia corporis forma*), Denzinger, *op. cit.* #1655. "The opinion which places in man one principle of life, namely the rational soul, from which the body also receives movement, and all life, and sense, is most common in the Church of God, and to many highly approved doctors it seems to be so intimately joined with the dogma of the Church that this is the sole legitimate, true interpretation of it, and hence not without error in faith could it be denied." Pius IX's letter, "Dolore haud mediocri," to the Bishop of Wratislawa, 30 April 1860. Denzinger, #1658. According to the Church of Cologne, "There can be no doubt that, according to the mind of the Council, all the operations of our life are accomplished by the rational soul itself created by God."

Prior to Clement's *De summa Trinitate et fide catholica* (6 May 1312), the Church's doctrine, as St. Thomas writes in his *Summa Contra Gentiles* I, 79 [15], was the teaching of Gennadius's *De ecclesisticis dogmatibus*, XVI, *Patrologia Latina*, 42, col. 1216: "The doctrine of the Catholic faith is in agreement on these matters. For in the work *On the Teachings of the Church* there is this statement: 'We believe that man alone is possessed of a subsistent soul, which continues to live even after divesting itself of the body, and is the animating principle of the senses

Descartes's conception of the soul does not accord with the official doctrine of the Church,[29] and in light of the decision of both the Vienne and Lateran Councils, it is enough to point out that his departure from the Church's doctrine amounts to heresy. If Descartes read the Bull,[30] he must have known what the Church's conception of the soul was. If he intended to use the Bull's contents to legitimize his own demonstration of the immortality of the soul (on the basis of the soul being distinct from the body), Descartes was using the papal document for purposes precisely contrary to those for which it was designed. In other words, either Descartes had not read the Bull, which is refuted by the evidence we have, or he deliberately decided to use the papal document to smuggle in his own conception under the mask of orthodoxy. Although Descartes was never accused of heresy on this count, one can say that the same Bull he used to legitimize his enterprise in the *Meditations* could well have been used against him.

III

In light of the above exposition, we should raise the familiar question concerning Descartes's sincerity. Did Descartes realize that he put forth the conception of the soul that the Church could not accept? "I have firm faith in the infallibility of the Church and in addition I have no doubts about my own arguments. I cannot have any fear that one truth may be in conflict with another," Descartes wrote to Mersenne.[31] If we take this statement at face value, it appears that Descartes believed in two things that seem to be mutually exclusive: the belief in the truth of his own doctrine and the Church's infallibility. Yet, in a certain interpretation the

and powers; nor does the soul die with the body, as the Arabian asserts, nor after a short period of time, as Zeno would have it, because it is a living substance.'"

30 In a letter to Regius, Descartes states: "I cannot approve . . . that 'men have a threefold soul.' In my religion this is an heretical thing to say; and quite apart from religion, it goes against logic. . . . Theologians indeed say that no created substance is the immediate principle of its operations . . ." May 1641 (AT III, 371–72; CSMK III, 182). It is likely that in writing these words, Descartes had in mind St. Thomas's discussion in *Summa Contra Gentiles*, II, 52.

31 Letter to Mersenne, December 1640 (AT III, 259; CSMK III, 161).

irreconcilability is only apparent. Twelve years after Descartes
published the *Meditations*, the Church condemned the doctrine of
Jansenius, in the Bull *Cum Occasione* (May 31, 1653), at the insti-
gation of the Jesuits. In condemning the doctrine of Jansenius, the
Church in fact condemned the doctrine of St. Augustine. To defend
the doctrine of St. Augustine, the Jansenists coined a distinction
between *question de droit* (*questio iuris*) and *question de fait*
(*questio facti*), that, as they believed, could save the Church from
an embarrassing situation. Accordingly, argued the Great Arnauld,
although the Church in fact condemned the "Five Propositions" as
heretical, these were not to be found in Jansenius's *Augustinus*. In
other words, the Pope did not condemn the doctrine of the great
saint but merely the propositions which the Jesuits presented to
the Holy Father.[32] This was another way of saying that the Pope
was led astray by the Jesuits in matters of facts (*question de fait*)
(le Pape n'ayant nullement condamnè ces sens [ou propositions]
particuliers, qui lui avoient étè exposés par ces Docteurs. . . . Sa
Sainteté ne les auroit point condamnés).[33] In short, the Pope,
though infallible in matters of faith (*question de droit*), can be fal-
lible in factual matters (*question de fait*).

To be sure, Descartes did not know the distinction between
question de droit and *question de fait*, and if the case of the
Jansenists is of any avail for our understanding of why Descartes
could see no contradiction in attacking the Scholastic formula
anima humanis corporis forma and declaring himself to be the
Church's obedient son, it is because the same psychological mechanism was at work. Just as the Jansenists were convinced of the
truth of St. Augustine's teaching on grace, Descartes was convinced
of the truth of his own doctrine: "It matters little to me whether I
am the first or the last to write what I write, provided that what I
write is true."[34] The Scholastic proposition *anima humanis*

---

32 See Leszek Kolakowski, *Dieu ne nous doit rien: Brève remarque sur la
    religion de Pascal et l'esprit du jansénisme* (Paris: Albin Michel, 1997),
    pp. 38–46.

33 "Relation Abrége sur le sujet des cinq Propositions condamnées par la
    Constitution du Pape Innocent X," in: *Oeuvres de Messire Antoine
    Arnauld*, vol. XIX (Paris, 1967), p. 78. Cf. "Argument du P. Annat, "*ibid.*,
    pp. 124–227.

34 Letter to [Vatier], 22 February 1638 (AT I, 562; CSMK III, 87).

corporis forma must have appeared in Descartes's eyes to be as remote from the truth as the semi-pelagian teaching of the Molinist Jesuits on freedom seemed to Arnauld and Pascal. The Jansenists knew that the Jesuits were introducing heresy into the bosom of the Church. The distinction between *question de droit* (*questio iuris*) and *question de fait* (*questio facti*) was of course useless as a theoretical tool, but it was a useful psychological device. It allowed one to believe that the Church is infallible despite its occasional deviations. One could always close one's eyes to the actual deviations and say that heresy entered the Church by accident.[35]

But how are we to distinguish which doctrine is a true doctrine and which is heretical? The Jansenists, in contrast to Descartes, were in a "comfortable" position. The theology of St. Augustine was a recognized pillar of Catholic theology, and even the Molinist Jesuits could not openly declare – without running the risk of destroying the binding force of tradition – that in condemning the doctrine of Jansenius they were in fact condemning the doctrine of St. Augustine. Tradition for Descartes was good only insofar as it provided edifying examples, but no truth properly speaking could be found in it. In rejecting tradition as the source of authority, all Descartes was left with was reason. His confidence in its power at times approached madness: "I think that the latter [traditional philosophy] would have been rejected as clashing with the Faith if mine had been known first."[36] In Descartes's eyes the doctrine of the Jesuits (the "followers of Aristotle") was thus as much a denial of truth as the semi-pelagianism was the denial of truth for the Jansenists. Not only does Descartes's position imply that the Church's teaching on the soul was false, but it also suggests that in reaffirming Clement V's position on the nature of the soul, the Pope Leo X himself was guilty of spreading heresy.

To declare what true doctrine was, independently of the

---

35 The dogma of papal infallibility was not known in the 17th century. F. Annat argues, however, that we owe obedience to the pope just because he is the pope: "même si le Pape n'était pas infaillible, il était le Pape, et il fallait lui obéir" (cited by Francis Ferrier, "Jansénius et Gibieuf, " in *L'augustinisme à l'ancienne faculté de théologie de Louvain*, ed. by M. Lambregts [Louvain: Louvain University Press, 1994], p. 65).

36 Letter to Mersenne, 31 March 1641 (AT III, 349–50; CSMK III, 177).

Church, could not be tolerated, though. When Pope Alexander VII in Bull *Ad sacram beati PETRI Sedem* (October 16, 1656) reaffirmed his predecessor's position on the five condemned propositions, the Holy See did away with the distinction between the *question de droit* and the *question de fait*, and implicitly asserted that the truth is identical with the official Church doctrine. In other words, there is no truth (with respect to matters of faith) independent of what the Church declares as such. This, of course, did not shake the belief of the Jansenists that Truth was on the side of St. Augustine (and theirs).

If Descartes had published the *Meditations* after October 16, 1656, and had still wished to stay in the Church, he would have had to give up his conviction, if sincere then certainly naive, that the doctrine of the followers of Aristotle was false. In 1641 he could still believe that there is a difference between truth and the official doctrine of the Church. Descartes's unshakable conviction that his was the (first) true philosophy is, I believe, the predominant reason that might explain his tacit opposition to the statement *anima humanis corporis forma*. In other words, it mattered little to Descartes that he was going against the official doctrine (this was for him a matter of tradition for which he had very little concern and respect); what mattered was the firm and sincere belief in the truth of one's own conception of the soul and, consequently, the conviction that every other conception must be false. I do not think more explanation is needed to understand why Descartes saw no contradiction between the truth of his own conception and the infallibility of the Catholic Church.

There is ample evidence in Descartes's correspondence that shows that he thought the Church doctrine was the same as that of the Jesuits.

> I will not travel during this winter, because in the next four or five months I am due to receive the objections of the Jesuits, and I think I should hold myself in readiness for them. Meanwhile I should like to reread some of their philosophy, which I have not looked at for twenty years.[37]

37 Letter to Mersenne, 30 September 1640 (AT III, 185; CSMK III, 153–54).

His war against the doctrines of the Jesuits was a battle of truth against falsehood in the name of the Christian Faith:

> So I have decided not to keep silent on this matter, and to fight with their own weapons the people who confound Aristotle with the Bible and abuse the authority of the Church in order to vent their passions – I mean the people who had Galileo condemned. They would have my views condemned likewise if they had the power; but if there is ever any question of that, I am confident I can show that none of the tenets of their philosophy accords with the Faith so well as my doctrines.[38]

Descartes did not have to be insincere when he wrote to Vatier that his philosophy (one truth) does not contradict the teaching of the Church (another truth); what it contradicted was simply the false doctrine of the "followers of Aristotle." The Pope's call on the philosophers to establish the truth of the soul served Descartes as a convenient excuse to destroy the Aristotelian conception in the name of the truth of one's own doctrine. If his doctrine was the true one, not only could he disregard the problem of heresy, but also to propose a new doctrine of the soul was imperative and pious.[39] This obsession with truth seems to be a key to understanding why Descartes could see no contradiction in believing in the infallibility of the Church on the one hand, and his own philosophy on the other.

IV

Be that as it may, the problem lay deeper, and it concerned the third of the condemned propositions: "truth never contradicts truth." As the publication of the *Meditations* approached, Descartes became more and more impatient. He insisted that Mersenne induce the Oratorian Guillaume Gibieuf (who had been a member of the Sorbonne since 1608) to seek the approbation for the *Meditations* among his colleagues on the Faculty of the

---

38   Letter to Mersenne, 31 March 1641 (AT III, 349–50; CSMK III, 177).

39   "I delayed [sending you my *Meditations*] because I do not want them to fall into the hands of pseudo-theologians or the Jesuits whom I foresee I shall have to fight – before I have had them seen and approved by various doctors, and if I can, by the Sorbonne as a whole." To Mersenne, 30 July 1640 (AT III, 126; CSMK III, 150).

University of Paris.[40] On November 11, 1640, Descartes rushed to explain personally to Gibieuf the content of his work.

> In my view, the route which I take to make known the nature of the human soul and to demonstrate the existence of God is the only one which could enable us to reach our destination. I am well aware that others could have made a much better job of following this path than I have, and that I will have left out much that needed to be explained; but I am sure that I can make good all the defects, provided that I am alerted to them, and that I can make the proofs I employ so evident and so certain that they can be taken as demonstrations. One problem none the less remains, which is that I cannot ensure that those of every level of intelligence will be capable of understanding the proofs. . . . Now I know of no people on earth who can accomplish more in this regard than the gentlemen of the Sorbonne, or anyone from whom I can expect a more sincere appraisal, and so I have decided to seek their special protection. And since you are one of the leading lights of the Society, and have always done me the honor of giving me signs of your affection, and above all since it is the cause of God that I have undertaken to defend, I have great hopes of your help in this matter.[41]

His correspondence with Mersenne makes it clear that there was more to the *Meditations* than merely "championing the cause of God" and proving the immortality of the soul. The same *Meditations* is a book on first philosophy; it contains the principles of a new physics, and it is supposed to destroy the foundations of Aristotelian physics by the time the reader concludes the Sixth

40 Cf. Letter to Mersenne, 30 September 1640 (AT III, 184, 1. 10–20; CSMK III, 153). It was assumed until recently that the approbation of the Sorbonne for the *Meditations* was never granted. Recently, J. Robert Armogathe convincingly argued on the basis of existing documents that the *Meditations* did receive the approbation. See his "L'approbation des Méditations par le Faculté de Théologie de Paris (1641)," in *Archives de Philosophie*, Bulletin Cartésien, XXI, 57, 1994 (1), pp. 1–3. For condemnations of Descartes's philosophy, see Jean-Robert Armogathe and Vincent Carraud, "La première condamnation des œuvres de Descartes, d'après des documents inédits aux archives du saint-office," in *Nouvelles de la République des Lettres*, 2001–II, pp. 103–37.

41 11 November 1640 (AT III, 237; CSMK III, pp. 157–58; cf. AT III, 237–38).

Meditation. The condemnation of Galileo dictated caution in proposing new physical theories; and there is nothing mysterious in that Descartes did not want this part of his enterprise to be known to others.

But was it only the doctrine of the Jesuits that Descartes tried to undermine, as he made himself, Mersenne and Gibieuf believe? The cornerstone of the new philosophy is the Universal Doubt; the immortality of the soul is demonstrated by casting doubt on the existence of the external world, including the doubter's own body. Likewise the existence of God: we know that God exists because God Himself implanted the idea of Himself in the human mind. The existence of God and the immortality of the soul are demonstrated by questioning the reliability of the human sensory apparatus. This means that there are no traces of God in the world, and, consequently, that none of St. Thomas's five ways (i.e., the cosmological argument) can be a reliable ladder leading from the external world to the Creator. In other words, in contradistinction to what St. Thomas and the Scholastics believed, and the Church taught, there is no path leading from the world to God, and, because the bodies may not exist, the soul cannot be *corporis forma*. The Papal Bull to which Descartes makes reference in his Letter to the Sorbonne was nothing but a practical weapon that Descartes very skillfully used in his game with the "followers of Aristotle."

How to Read Descartes's
First Meditation:
The Place of the Doctrine of the Eternal
Truths in the First Meditation[1]

Despite the existence of the enormous exegetic literature on the *Meditations*, in which Descartes's every step has been subjected many times to meticulous analysis by Cartesian scholars, surprisingly enough, there is no systematic analysis of the second part of the First Meditation: AT VII, 21–23; CSM, II, 14–15.[2] Let me quote this part.

> [1]
> And yet firmly rooted in my mind is the long-standing opinion that there is an omnipotent God who made me the kind of creature that I am. How do I know that he has not brought it about that there is no earth, no sky, no extended

1 This chapter is a considerably revised version of the article which was originally published in *The Southern Journal of Philosophy*, Vol. XXXV, 1997. Upon its publication, my article met with criticism by Georges Moyal ("Descartes, Mathematics, and Atheists: A Reply to Zbigniew Janowski," Vol. XXXVII, 1999). Although my reading of the First Meditation changed considerably, I still maintain the core of my argument about the "Epicurean" structure of Descartes's argument. The main difference between the former and present version is the inclusion of the entire section on the possible place of the eternal truths doctrine in the First Meditation.

2 One should consult the brief but insightful account in Stefano Di Bella, *Meditazioni metafisiche: Introduzione alla lettura* (Rome: NIS, 1997), pp. 53–57.

thing, no shape, no size, no place, while at the same time ensuring that all these things appear to me to exist just as they do now? What is more, since I sometimes believe that others go astray in cases where they think they have the most perfect knowledge, may I not similarly go wrong every time I add two and three or count the sides of a square, or in some even simpler matter, if that is imaginable.

[1A]

But perhaps God would not have allowed me to be deceived in this way since he is said to be supremely good. But if it were inconsistent with his goodness to have created me such that I am deceived all the time, it would seem equally foreign to his goodness to allow me to be deceived even occasionally; yet this last assertion cannot be made.

[2]

But there might perhaps be some people (*nonnulli qui*) who would prefer to deny the existence of a God so powerful than to believe that all other things are uncertain. These people might suppose that I have come by fate, or by chance, or by a continuous series of things (*seu fato, seu casu, seu continuata rerum serie*), or by whatever other means that you will, to be that which I am. Because to be deceived and to err seem to be certain imperfections, the less powerful an author of my origin these people will assign, the more likely it is that I am so imperfect as to be deceived all the time. [The French version reads: Let us not oppose them for a moment and grant them that everything said about God is a fable.] I have no answer to these arguments, but am finally compelled to admit that there is not one of my former beliefs about which a doubt may not properly be raised; and this is not a flippant or ill-considered conclusion, but is based on powerful and well thought-out reasons. So in future I must withhold my assent from these former beliefs just as carefully as I would from obvious falsehoods if I want to discover any certainty.

[3]

But it is not enough merely to have noticed this; I must make an effort to remember it. My habitual opinions keep coming back, and, despite my wishes, they capture my belief, which is as it were bound over to them as a result of long occupation and the law of custom. I shall never get out of the habit of confidently assenting to these opinions, so long as I suppose them to be what in fact they are, namely highly probable opinions — opinions which, despite the fact that they are in a sense doubtful, as has just been shown, it is still much more reasonable to believe than to deny. In view of this, I think it will be a good plan to turn my will in completely the opposite direction and deceive myself, by pretending for a time that these former opinions are utterly false and imaginary. I shall do this until the weight of preconceived opinion is counter-balanced and the distorting influence of habit no longer prevents my judgment from perceiving things correctly. In the meantime, I know that no danger or error will result from my plan, and that I cannot possibly go too far in my distrustful attitude. This is because the task now in hand does not involve action but merely the acquisition of knowledge.

[4]
I will suppose therefore that not God, who is supremely good and the source of truth, but rather some malicious demon of the utmost power and cunning (*summe potentem & callidum/non moins rusè et trompeur que puissant*) has employed all his energies in order to deceive me. I shall think that the sky, the air, the earth, colors, shapes, sounds and all external things are merely the delusions of dreams which he has devised to ensnare my judgment . . .

It is customary to link Descartes's considerations from paragraph [1] with those in paragraph [4] almost completely ignoring the contents of paragraphs [1A][3], [2] and [3]. What encourages this practice of passing over paragraphs [1A], [2] and [3] is the smooth thematical passage between paragraphs [1] and [4]. While in the first passage ([1]) Descartes suggests that I cannot be certain that God did not make it so that I am deceived in believing that the world really exists and that $2 + 3 = 5$, in the second passage ([4]), he makes an explicit supposition that I am deceived by the evil genius.

At first glance there seems indeed to be a direct link between paragraphs [1] and [4], whereas paragraphs [1A], [2] and [3] – where the discussion strays away from the hypothesis of the

3   The division into [1] and [1A] is mine.

deceiver — form the impression of being a disturbing insertion into an otherwise complete train of thought. Accordingly, "The hypothesis of the evil genius is substituted for that of the deceitful God simply because it is less offensive," Anthony Kenny writes. "The content of the two hypotheses is the same, namely, that an omnipotent deceiver is trying to deceive. . . ."[4] "The evil genius [is an] imaginary being on whom Descartes has conferred the omnipotence of God without His goodness."[5] The weakness of Kenny's "prudential" explanation is that it runs counter to Descartes's own explanation in the First Meditation (paragraph [2]), in his *Replies to the Sixth Set of Objections*,[6] and in his 1647 letter to the Curators of Leiden University.[7] Whatever one's final judgment regarding the differences between the two hypotheses,[8] what

4   Anthony Kenny, *Descartes* (New York: Random House, 1986; South Bend, Ind.: St. Augustine's Press, 2007), p. 35. This reading is shared by almost all major Descartes scholars: Ferdinand Alquié, *La Découverte métaphysique de l'homme chez Descartes* (Paris: Presses Universitaire de France, 1945), p. 177; cf. his [undated] Sorbonne lectures *Science et métaphysique chez Descartes* (Paris: Centre de Documentation Universitaire), p. 58.; L. J. Beck, *The Metaphysics of Descartes: A Study of the Meditations* (Westport, Conn.: Greenwood Press, 1965), pp. 57–58); and *Histoire de la philosophie*, vol. I, part 3 (Paris: PUF, 1967 ed); Harry Frankfurt, *Demons, Dreamers, and Madmen: The Defense of Reason in Descartes's Meditations* (Indianapolis: The Bobbs-Merrill Company, 1970), pp. 68–69, 87; Étienne Gilson, *Études sur le rôle de la pensée médiévale dans la formation du systéme cartésien* (Paris: Librairie Philosophique J. Vrin, 1930), 3rd ed., 1967, p. 235–36; Anthony Kenny, *Descartes* [New York: Random House, 1986; South Bend, Ind.: St. Augustine's Press, 2008], p. 35); Jean Laporte (*Le rationalisme de Descartes* (Paris: Presses Universitaires de France, 1945), p. 172; Margaret Dauler Wilson, *Descartes* (London: Routledge & Kegan Paul, 1978), p. 34.
5   Émile Bréhier, *La philosophie et son passé* (Paris: PUF, 1940), p. 114.
6   AT VII, 428, CSM II, 289.
7   AT V 8, CSMK III, 316.
8   Several decades ago Henri Gouhier, *Descartes: Essais* (Paris: Vrin, 1949), pp. 143–75, pointed out that mathematics is missing from the list of items the evil genius renders dubitable. More recently, Richard Kennington in "The Finitude of Descartes' Evil Genius," *Journal of the History of Ideas*, 32 (1971), pp. 441–46, noticed that Descartes does not refer to the evil genius as "omnipotent" (*omnipotens*), but only as "extremely powerful" (*summe potens*). From the fact that the genius is less than omnipotent

remains unexplained is, first, why Descartes changed the *ratio dubitandi*, and, second, what is the role of the middle paragraphs (especially paragraph [2]).

It is my contention that (1) the doctrine of eternal truths constitutes the invisible spine of the *deus deceptor* hypothesis and (2) that the function of the intermediate paragraph [2], where Descartes invokes "some people" (*nonnulli qui*) "who would prefer to deny the existence of a God so powerful," is to show the weakness of the atheist position vis-à-vis his conception of God known as the doctrine of the eternal truths which Descartes formulated to combat atheism.[9]

I

The starting point of Descartes's considerations in paragraph [1] is the *vetus opinio* ("a long-standing opinion"), according to which, there is a God. This God, Descartes says, can do everything (*potest omnia*). He can make it so there is "no earth, no sky, no extended thing, no shape, no size, no place, while at the same time ensuring that all these things appear to me to exist just as they do now."[10] In other words, God could make it so that there is nothing outside me – or, rather, one should say outside my mind, since the non-existence of heaven and earth, etc. would also cause the non-existence of my body – and yet I would perceive everything as if it existed. Both Descartes's language and the first two items from the

Kennington infers that the doubt was never intended to include mathematics. Kennington's position was criticized by Hiram Caton in "Kennington on Descartes' Evil Genius," *Journal of the History of Ideas*, 34 (1973), pp. 639–41; see the reply by Kennington, *ibid.*, pp. 641–43, and Caton's "Rejoinder: The Cunning of the Evil Demon," *ibid.*, pp. 643–44. It should be noted that in his article Kennington does not mention Descartes's letter to the Curators of Leiden University, in which the philosopher does not make use of the distinction between *summe potens* and *omnipotens* on which Kennington's thesis is based.

9   See, for example, Descartes' s letter to Mersenne, 6 May 1630, AT I, 149; CSMK III, 24.

10 Mark Olson in his very interesting study of the First Meditation, "Descartes' First Meditation: Mathematics and the Laws of Logic" (*Journal of the History of Philosophy*, 26 [July 1988], p. 427), convincingly argues that this passage is Descartes's critique of Saint Thomas' theory of abstraction, which "paves the way for the Ontological argument."

list – earth and sky – bring to mind, and almost certainly brought to the mind of Descartes's contemporaries, the words of the Nicene Creed: *Credo in Deum Patrem Omnipotentem, Creatorem cœli et terre, etc.* (I believe in God, Father Almighty, the Creator of Heaven and Earth, etc). The *vetus opinio* is clearly a reference to the Biblical God-the-creator.[11]

Up to this point Descartes's argument does not go beyond very well-known sceptical considerations. In construing the first part of the *deus deceptor* hypothesis Descartes could very well have used old skeptical argument.

The second part of Descartes's hypothesis is much more original: God can also make it so that I would go wrong even when I add two plus three. Three interrelated questions arise here.

– First, given the fact that Descartes never offers a single example of being deceived in mathematics, what reason does he have to entertain such a possibility? And how is deception in the mathematical realm supposed to be understood?

– Second, how can he legitimate the move from being deceived in the sensory realm to being deceived in the realm of simple essences.

– Third, why had no thinker before Descartes entertained the possibility of mathematics being dubitable, whereas a host of them used skeptical arguments, including the possibility of being deceived by God?[12]

---

11   Such a reading is also upheld by Stefano Di Bella, *Meditazioni metafisiche: Introduzione alla lettura* (Rome: NIS, 1997), p. 52. Di Bella rightly adds that Descartes's use of the God of the Creed ("Dio del Credo") is not merely a simple reference to "common belief," but much "more sophisticated theological *opinion*" (emphasis in the original).

12   The text of Cicero *Academica*, II, xv, 47, reads: "They first attempt to show the possibility that many things may appear to exist that are absolutely non-existent, since the mind is deceptively affected by non-existent objects in the same manner as it is affected by the real ones. For, they say, when your school asserts that some presentations are sent by the deity – dreams for example, and the revelations furnished by oracles, auspices and sacrifices (for they assert that the Stoics against whom they are arguing accept these manifestations) – how possibly, they ask, can the deity have the power to render false presentations probable and not have the power to render probable those which approximate absolutely most

As far as the first and second questions are concerned, the answer is the following: assuming that an omnipotent and benevolent God created my cognitive apparatus, it is unclear why the sensory apparatus is (*interdum*) deceptive. From this Descartes moves on to make a supposition that my perceptions of the external world might not come from objects that actually exist outside of me, but can be the projection of my mind by means of ideas which God can put in my mind. Hence the conclusion that an omnipotent God could make it so that what I perceive to be the world might in fact not exist outside of me but merely *appear* to exist.

closely to the truth?" To my knowledge no Descartes scholar has entertained the idea that, perhaps, Descartes read Plutarch's *The Contradictions of the Stoics*, where we find the following passage: "In their conflict with the Academics the effort of Chrysippus and Antipater concerns the following: there is no action nor the [act of the] will without assent, but it is a fiction and a vain hypothesis to believe that . . . the will acts right away without having conceded and given assent to this representation. Moreover, what Chrysippus and Antipater exerted themselves over most in their fight against the Academics [was] the doctrine that '*one does neither act nor move toward something without previously assenting, and it is pure imagination and a vain hypothesis on the part of those who think that, having had an adequate representation, one immediately moves toward something without yielding or assenting to the representation.*" And: "According to Chrysippus, both God and the wise man [*sapientes* – Cf. Cicero, *Academica* II, xxiv, 78 – Z.J.] induce false representations, desiring that we not assent or yield [to them], but solely act and move toward what appears to us; and that we, being foolish, [or] out of weakness assent to such representations. It is in no way difficult to see the confusion and the reciprocal disagreement that these statements betray; indeed whoever – God or wise men – does not desire that those to whom he provides representations, assent [to the latter], but rather that they act, knows that the representation is sufficient to act, but the assent is superfluous; but if he produces false and persuasive representations instead, because he thinks that a representation without assent does not bring about a movement toward action, then he is the voluntary cause of the fact that humans act recklessly and are in error because they assent to representations that do not apprehend reality. . . . But that which he [Chrysippus] says with such force of the representations," Plutarch continues, "contradicts the idea that Fatum hovers over everything. To demonstrate that a representation (*phantasia*) is not the complete cause of the assent, he says that wise men who create false representations would be harmful if the representations were the total cause of the assent. . . . If one transposes this [reasoning] from the wise men to

Note here, to account for the non-existence of the external world Descartes did not need to seek recourse to the hypothesis of the deceiving God; the traditional skeptical arguments (including the example of the madman which Descartes invokes earlier) would suffice here. Why, then, did he introduce here the *persona* of God as a *ratio dubitandi*? The simplest answer is this: no traditional skeptical argument can render mathematics dubitable,[13] whereas an omnipotent God can. Descartes's argument is as follows: human cognitive apparatus is of one piece, regardless of whether it operates in the realm of sensory perceptions or mathematical essences; if God would deceive me in the sensory realm, one should assume that He could deceive me in mathematics as well. It has been noted many times that the *deus deceptor* hypothesis requires that to render mathematics dubitable God's power must be divorced from the restraints that benevolence imposes on it – since an omnipotent but good God would not deceive me. However, this explanation does not take into account one thing: it is one thing to wish to deceive; it is another to have the power to do so. In other words, is God powerful *enough* to deceive me in the realm of mathematics? And if so, does Descartes mean that God could make me think that 2 + 3 might be, say, 55?

Descartes does not make explicit what deception in the mathematical realm would mean. One way to understand it is to assume that God could deceive him by making him think, for example, 2 +

Destiny, and if one says then that assents are not due to Destiny because [if] the assents and the false judgments and errors would be due to it, Destiny would be harmful to us. The same reason which contradicts that the wise man is harmful shows at the same time that Destiny is not the cause of everything." Latin text in Plutarch, *Stoicorum repugnantis*, in *Plutarchi Chaeronensis*, ed. by Iacobus Reiski, vol. 10, Lipsiae (1878). The English translation, Plutarch, *Stoic Self-Contradictions*, in *Moralia*, tr. by Harold Cherniss (Cambridge: Harvard University Press, Loeb Classical Library, 1976), vol. XII, part II.

 For references to St. Augustine's use of skeptical arguments, see my *Augustinian-Cartesian Index: Texts and Commentary* (South Bend, Ind.: St. Augustine's Press, 2004).

13 *Meditazioni metafisiche de Descartes* (Rome: Editori Laterza, 1997), p. 27. I discuss this question with reference to St. Thomas in my *Cartesian Theodicy* (Dortrecht/Boston: Kluwer, 2000), chapter 3.

3 = 55. Deception as normally understood is a state in which one's perception of reality has been temporarily obstructed. A straight rod immersed in water is perceived as bent; the sun appears small, although it is large; a rectangular tower looks round from afar. I can say, as Descartes does, that I was deceived when I saw a straight rod bent in water, because the rod is actually straight, etc. In other words, the concept of deception presupposes a *hard reality*, independent of my perception of it, against which I can verify my perceptions. The case of mathematics is different, however. There is no "space," so to speak, between the object of my perception, i.e., mathematical essences, and my mind, as in the case of a rod immersed in water and my eyes, or the tower seen from afar. If by deception Descartes means that God could change the truth value of 2 + 3 into, say, 55, deception would be virtually undetectable since He would make me think in one instance that 2 + 3 = 5 and at another instance 55. In each case the result would be what my mind necessarily assents to at a given moment, 5 or 55, and the question of whether 2 + 3 = 5 or 55 could not even arise. The implication is clear: to change 2 + 3 into 55 would require that eternal verities be subject to divine legislation.

If Descartes in fact thought that God could deceive him by making him think that the result of 2 + 3 could be other than 5, then the *deus deceptor* requires that eternal verities can be other than what we know them to be. Can they? None of Descartes's predecessors entertained the hypothesis that we can cast doubt on mathematics. As Emanuela Scribano put it, the argument is "unimaginable" from the point of view of classical skepticism. The Scholastic God, for example, is not free *not* to abide by truths of logic and mathematics. Take, for example, the following passage from St. Thomas Aquinas's *Summa Theologica*, Q. 16. Art. 7:

> It seems that created truths are eternal. For Augustine says in De Libero Arbitrio, *Nothing is more eternal than the nature of a circle, and that two added to three make five.* But the truth of these is a created truth. Therefore created truth is eternal (*Videtur quod veritas creata sit aeterna. Dicit enim Augustinus, in* De Libero arbitrio, *quod nihil est magis aeternum quam ratio circuli, et duo et tria esse*

quinque. Sed horum veritatis est veritas creata. Ergo ver-
itas creata est aeterna).

Reply 1: The nature of a circle, and the fact that two and
three make five, have eternity in the mind of God (*Ergo*
dicendum quod ratio circuli, et duo et tria esse quinque
habent aeternitatem in mente divina).

From Aquinas's perspective the *deus deceptor* hypothesis requires
that mathematical essences are not "in" the Divine mind; if they
are "in" it, God is "constrained" by them, so to speak.[14]

Descartes strongly denies any differentiation, even conceptual,
between Divine intellect and Divine will: "nor should we conceive
any precedence between His intellect and His will. . . . This is well
expressed by the words of St. Augustine: 'They are so because
Thou see'est them to be so' because in God seeing (*videre*) and
willing (*velle*) are one and the same thing."[15] And in the *Sixth Set*
of Replies to the Meditations Descartes makes this point even more
emphatic, positioning himself explicitly against the Scholastics:
"There is not even the priority of order (*prius fuit ordine*), or tem-
poral priority (*priorite temporis*), or of 'rationally determined reason' (*ratio-rationitata*) as they [the Schoolmen] call it, such that
God's idea of the good impelled him to choose one thing rather
than another."[16]

Although Descartes does not name any specific Schoolman,
several passages from the *Summa Contra Gentiles*, I, 8, might
establish Aquinas as the opponent Descartes had in mind: "the
apprehended good determines the will as its proper object." And in
the same work, II, 23, Aquinas states that an agent acting "for an
end must act by intellect and will." (Aquinas differentiates between
will and intellect in God to counteract "the error of those who say
that all things depend on the simple will of God, without any

14 This is what Descartes thought when he used the Styx/Fates metaphor in
    his Letter to Mersenne (15 April 1630; AT I, 145, CSMK III, 23) and in his
    Fifth Set of Replies (AT VII, 380; CSM II, 261).
15 To Mesland, May 2, 1644 (AT IV, 119; CSMK III, 235.
16 *Sixth Set of Replies* (AT VII, 432; CSM II, 291; cf. Leibniz, *Theodicy*,
    para.191.

reason"; SCG, II, 24).[17] Aquinas is by no means the only Medieval whom Descartes could think of. Ockham's God "looks to [ideas] in producing, and is precisely called rational creator (*Deus est ratio-nabiliter operans*) because he produces by looking at them."[18]

What possible advantage might such a conception of God have over the God of the Schoolmen? First and foremost, Descartes conceived the doctrine of eternal truths as a practical weapon against atheism. After explaining to Mersenne the metaphysical underpinnings of the doctrine, Descartes states: "we must not say that 'if God did not exist nevertheless these truths would be true. . . . It is easy to be mistaken about this because most people do not regard God as a being who is infinite and beyond our grasp, *the sole author on whom all things depend.*"[19] Accordingly, the perfect simplicity of God's nature, where there is no room for the distinction between intellect and will, precludes the possibility of the eternal truths being "in" God's intellect; hence the conclusion that insofar as those truths are not dependent on man's mind, they must depend on God who is also their creator.[20] Thus the atheist's denial of God's existence is tantamount to reducing them to psychological rules governing our thinking,[21] or *persvasio*, as

---

17 I discuss Aquinas's (and Ockham's) conception of God in relation to Descartes's own conception in my *Cartesian Theodicy, op. cit.,* pp. 97–106.

18 Ockham, *Commentary on the First Book of Sentences.* In *Ockham: Studies and Selections.* Edited by Stephen Chak Tornay (LaSalle, Ill.: The Open Court Publishing Company, 1938), p. 492.

19 AT I, 150; CSMK II, 24–25.

20 Letter to Mersenne, 27 May 1630, AT I, 151, CSMK III, 25.

21 According to one story, before his death, when asked to make a confession of faith, the Prince of Nassau responded: "I believe that 2 + 2 = 4, and that 4 + 4 = 8." (Geneviève Rodis-Lewis, *Descartes* [Paris: Calmann-Lévy, 1995], p. 94. For a more detailed account, see Richard Watson, *Cogito, Ergo Sum: The Life of René Descartes* [Boston: David R. Godine Publisher, 2002], p. 30.) The philosophical "moral" of atheist "confession of faith" is that one can deny the existence of God without losing faith in the absolute certainty of mathematics. The story was apparently very well known, which is testified by the fact that Molière put Nassau's words in the mouth of his Don Juan. Descartes served in Nassau's army, and it is probable that he had the Prince in mind when he construed the doctrine of eternal truths.

Descartes explained in his exchange with the objectors to the *Meditations*.[22]

The authors of the *Second Set of Objections*, noted:

> The fourth difficulty concerns the kind of knowledge possessed by an atheist. When the atheist asserts "If equals are taken from equals the remainder will be equal" or "the three angles of a rectilinear triangle are equal to two right angles" and numerous similar propositions . . . [which are] very certain and indeed – on your own criterion – utterly evident. He maintains that this is so true that even if God does not exist and is not even possible (as he believes), he is just as certain of these truths as if God really existed. Moreover he maintains that no reason for doubt can be presented to him that could shake him in the slightest or make him at all uncertain. What reason can you produce [to shake his conviction]?[23]

In response Descartes (following St. Augustine[24]) wrote:

> The fact that an atheist can be clearly aware that the three angles of a triangle are equal to two right angles is something I do not dispute. But I maintain that this *awareness* of his is not true knowledge, since no act of awareness that can be rendered doubtful seems fit to be called *knowledge*. Now since we are supposing that this individual is an atheist, he cannot be certain that he is not being deceived on matters that seem to him to be very evident (as I fully explained).[25]

"Without doubt," Henri Gouhier writes, "one can read the *Discourse on the Method*, the six *Meditations*, the *Principles of Philosophy* without finding an *explicit* exposition of the doctrine of the eternal truths."[26] To be sure, there are no explicit references to this doctrine, but one can express certain doubts about there being

22 AT VII, 417–18, CSM II, 281; AT VII, 379–80, CSM II, 261.
23 AT VII, 414–15; CSM II, 279.
24 The distinction between *scientia* and *persvasio* comes from *De quantitate animae*, XXX, 58. See my *Augustinian-Cartesian Index*, op. cit.., p. 112.
25 *Second Set of Replies*. AT VII 141, CSM II, 279.
26 Henri Gouhier, *Cartèsianisme et augustinisme au XVIIe siècle* (Paris: Vrin, 1978), p. 157 (emphasis mine).

no exposition, however implicit,[27] of this doctrine in the *Meditations*. In the First Meditation, Descartes addresses the *same* concern which the authors of the *Sixth Set of Objections* addressed: "[S]ince I sometimes believe that others go astray in cases where they think they have the most perfect knowledge, may I not similarly go wrong every time I add two and three or count the sides of a square, or in some even simpler matter, if that is imaginable." In his letter to Regius, Descartes repeats this sentence almost verbatim: ". . . *perhaps* our nature is such that we go wrong even in the most evident matters."[28] And he continues, bringing in the explanation that he offered in his *Second Set of Replies*:

> There is a *conviction* when there remains some reason that might lead us to doubt, but *knowledge* is a conviction based

27 Some readers of the *Meditations*, most notably Gassendi and the authors of the *Sixth Set of Objections* realized that 4 + 4 = 8 is, according to Descartes, a truth established by God. The text that drew Gassendi's attention is the following passage from the Fourth Meditation:

> Even if perhaps no such figure [as a triangle] exists, or has never existed, anywhere outside my thought, there is still a determinate nature that is not invented by me or dependent on my mind. . . . And since these properties are ones that I now clearly and distinctly recognized, whether I want to or not . . . it follows that they cannot have been invented by me.

Here is Gassendi's reaction:

> But this is just hard to accept and in any case it is impossible to grasp how there can be a human nature [or a nature of a triangle] if no human being [or a triangle] exists. . . . The schoolmen say that talking of the essence of things is one thing and talking about their existence is another, and that although things do not exist from eternity, their essences are eternal. But in that case, does God do anything very impressive when He produces their existence? Is He doing any more than a tailor does when he tries a suit of clothes on someone? How can people defend the thesis that the essence of man . . . is eternal and independent of God. . . , the same applies to your triangle and its nature. The triangle is a kind of mental rule that you use to find out whether something deserves to be called a triangle. But we should not therefore say that such a triangle is something real, or that it is a true nature distinct from intellect. *Fifth Set of Objections*. AT VII, 319–21; CSM II, 222–23.

28 Letter to Regius, 24 May 1640 (AT III, 64, CSMK III, 147), emphasis Z.J.

on a reason so strong that it can never be shaken by any stronger reason. Nobody can have the latter unless he also has knowledge of God. But a man who has once clearly understood the reasons that convince us that God exists and is not a deceiver . . . will continue to possess not only the conviction, but real knowledge . . .

If we apply the language of the *Replies* and of the letter to Regius to the *deus deceptor* hypothesis, Descartes's question can be reformulated in the following way: is 2 + 3 = 5 *scientia* or mere *persvasio*.[29] And if it is *persvasio*, what is the procedure for turning it into *scientia*? The letter to Regius and the *deus deceptor* hypothesis make clear that in order to transform *persvasio* into *scientia* I need to invoke the hypothesis of the deceiving God, and subsequently undermine it.

The distinction between *persvasio* and *scientia* which we find in Descartes's *Second Set of Replies* and in his letter to Regius is, I believe, the missing link which connects the metaphysics of the *Meditations* with the foundational doctrine of the eternal truths as Descartes formulated it in his three letters to Mersenne in 1630.[30]

29 The immediate implication of the idea that the external world may not exist is that it entails that other people, and thus other minds, do not exist either. Now, if I am the only being aware of his existence, then the rules of my thinking (mathematics) are not an objective set of logical norms, but are the "psychological" rules of the way in which *my* mind functions. Thus what I think to be indubitable (2 + 3 = 5) is in the final analysis nothing but the rules of *my* mind. The weakness of this interpretation is that it implies that in order to validate mathematics Descartes would have to appeal to common agreement. However, no common agreement will do here. One can imagine a state of collective solipsism where everyone's experience of reality is the same, yet, it is false in the absolute sense.

30 To my knowledge only Martial Gueroult makes the claim that the deceiving God hypothesis is connected with the eternal truths doctrine. "The opposition between the evil genius and the veracious God then appears as the reflection of a kind of conflict between his power and his goodness, between his power and his will: God being capable of deceiving us, but not wanting to. From this stems the identification of the roots of this hypothesis with the theory of eternal truths: God was as free to deceive us as he was free to create truths other than those we recognize, to the extent that it could have been true that the sum of the angles of a triangle were not equal to two right angles, and two plus three not equal five." *Descartes' Philosophy Interpreted According to the Order of Reasons*, vol. I, *The*

II

Be that as it may, one can ask the following question: what reason do I have to suppose that God can deceive me? In [1A] Descartes states that God would not allow that I would be deceived, *since* "he is said to be supremely good." Yet having said this, Descartes makes the following observation: "if it were inconsistent with his goodness to have created me such that I am deceived all the time, it would seem equally foreign to his goodness to allow me to be deceived even occasionally." Unlike in paragraph [1], in which "to be deceived" means that God Himself makes me think something while it is not the case (e.g., that there is a sky and earth while there is neither a sky nor an earth), in paragraph [1A] "to be deceived" means to have a nature which makes me erroneously assert something. While in [1] Descartes works on the assumption that it is God who is the source of my erroneously asserting something to be the case, in [1A] Descartes shifts the problem of deception to my having such a nature that deceives itself. (The French translation employs here the reflexive verb *se tromper*, to deceive oneself, which better fits the interpretation according to which it is my nature which is prone to error.)

As for the argument itself, Descartes's point is the following: as far as God's goodness is concerned, it does not matter whether God gave me a nature that makes me always (*semper*) go wrong, or only sometimes (*interdum*). In other words, if God is omnipotent He could create a human cognitive nature which never goes wrong; if He is good, He would have given me the nature that does not go wrong even sometimes. Here is, however, the difficulty: When, for example, I go wrong every fifth or tenth time, I can say that I "sometimes" go wrong. But would my going wrong once in a million cases also qualify as "sometimes"? The problem here is, clearly, conceptual. However, in working out his methodology at the very outset of the *Meditations* Descartes made it his rule "not to confide completely in those who deceived us even once,"[31] and therefore we should take the term "sometimes" to mean in this context "never." Thus to cast doubt on God's goodness it is enough

Soul and God, tr. by Roger Ariew (Minneapolis: University of Minnesota Press, 1984), p. 22.
31   AT VII, 18, CSM II, 17; emphasis mine.

if I go wrong only once. The logic of the argument is the proverbial "everything or nothing": only my *never* going wrong is "not repugnant" to God's goodness; while even a single instance of my going wrong is inconsistent with it. It would seem that by casting doubt on God's goodness Descartes is stripping God of His goodness and thus he is preparing ground for the introduction of an omnipotent but evil genius.

Now, why at this point does Descartes not introduce the evil genius, but rather the *nonnulli qui* (some people), who deny the existence of God+ Why didn't Descartes move directly from paragraph [1A] to [4]? Let us have a closer look at the intermediate passages. Rather than opening the new paragraph with the introduction of the "less offensive" hypothesis of the evil genius, Descartes invokes "some people" (*nonnulli qui*). All of a sudden Descartes's hitherto solitary meditation takes on the form of a polemic. The appearance of "some people" seems to be a *deus ex machina*; neither is it immediately clear why Descartes introduces them, who they are, nor what they have to do with the immediately preceding considerations concerning the existence or non-existence of the external world, the certainty of mathematics, and God's role in the fact that I go wrong.

Martial Gueroult and Jean-Marie Beyssade, who have briefly commented upon this passage, claim the *nonnulli qui* to be atheists; Georges Moyal qualified this claim arguing that the *nonnulli qui* are atheist mathematicians.[32] Considering the fact that the dubitability of mathematics is the subject matter of the hypothesis of the deceiver ([1]), Moyal's interpretation is indeed tempting. Yet before we accept it we should consider a few more points which are raised in Descartes's account. Neither Gueroult and Beyssade on the one hand nor Moyal on the other explain, first, why Descartes

---

32 Martial Gueroult, *Descartes' Philosophy Interpreted according to the Order of Reason*, vol. I, *The Soul and God*, tr. by Roger Ariew (Minneapolis: University of Minnesota Press, 1984), p. 24; Jean-Marie Beyssade, "'Devenir athées.' Sur un passage controversé de la Première Méditation," *Archives de Philosophie* (Bulletin Cartésien, XX), vol. 55 (1992), pp. 3–6. Cf. his *La philosophie première de Descartes* (Paris: Flammarion, 1979), pp. 87–89; Georges J. D. Moyal, "Veritas aeterna, Deo volente," *Les Etudes philosophiques*, 4 (1987), pp. 470, 474.

uses here the vague and imprecise term *nonnulli qui* instead of the common term *athei* which he employs in the *Letter to the Sorbonne* in spelling out the apologetic character of his work. Also, what remains unexplained is how did the *nonnulli qui* find their way into paragraph [2].

Descartes's hypothesis of *deus deceptor* reveals a structural similarity with the famous Epicurean argument: If there is evil, then God is either evil or impotent or both.[33] This argument can be reformulated into Cartesian epistemological categories: since I am *occasionally* deceived (deception, as Descartes says in the Fourth Meditation, leads to sin), then either God deceives me (in which case He is evil), or He is impotent (if he gave me a nature which goes wrong) or both. This objection is, of course, very difficult to refute. One cannot convincingly argue that an omnipotent God

33 Ever since the heresies of the Manicheans and the Bulgarian Bogomils, which permeated Western Christendom as the heresies of the Cathars and Albigiensies, the existence of an evil deity had not been a problem, and it is highly unlikely that Descartes was trying to resurrect it in the *Meditations*. What had been a problem, however, and was very much alive in Descartes's time, was the atheism associated in the sixteenth and seventeenth centuries almost exclusively with the spread of Epicurean ideas. "The movement of intellectual disbelief was manifested in, if not caused directly by, revivals of ancient philosophies of the Epicurean, Stratovian, Stoical and Lucretial kinds. There were, in consequence, few tracts against atheism that did not rebut the Epicurean premises concerning chance and the formation of the world, the eternity of matter, or the non-existence of Providence. . . . Whereas the religious turned to Cicero and endlessly quoted from his *De Natura Deorum*, whilst they thumbed through Ovid and cited their Seneca, their opponents turned to the *De Rerum natura* or to modern versions of its contents" (John Redwood, *Reason, Ridicule and Religion: The Age of Enlightenment in England 1660–1750* [London: Thames and Hudson, 1976], p. 40), and: "[Atheism] in 1613 was not identified with seminal thinkers or critically current philosophies, it was a revival; its names [Diagoras of Melos, Protagoras, Theodore of Cyrene, Bion of Borysthenes, Lucian] were standard names of antiquity. . . . The immanent materialism of the Epicureans could provide fuel for its fires" (Michael J. Buckley, S.J., *At the Origins of Modern Atheism* [New Haven & London: Yale University Press, 1987], pp. 46–47). "For many seventeenth- and eighteenth-century writers atheism seems to have been essentially connected with almost animistic chance theory." (David Berman, *A History of Atheism in Britain: From Hobbes to Russell* [London: Croom Helm, 1988], p. 44.)

could create man's nature in such a way that he would *never* go wrong, and yet He created it as He did. A God who could prevent evil but did not would be responsible for the existence of evil. What is more, if God had power to create me in such a way that I would never go wrong but did not do it, how do I know that He in fact is all-powerful? Or, to push this reasoning to its extreme, how do I know that God exists at all? In other words, as the existence of evil for the Epicureans was a reason to reject the existence of god(s), man's liability to error plays a similar role in Descartes's argument: it suspends not only belief in the goodness of God but puts in question marks His existence as well.

Are the *nonnulli qui* atheist Epicureans, as I suggested, or atheists, as Gueroult and Beyssade believe, or atheist mathematicians, as Moyal argues? In the second sentence in this paragraph, Descartes provides additional information which makes the problem of their precise identification even more complicated. These people, Descartes states, believe that "I have come by fate, or by chance, or by a continuous series of things (*seu fato, seu casu, seu continuata rerum serie*), or by whatever other means that you will, to be that which I am." In other words, according to *nonnulli qui* human (cognitive) nature was not created by God – but originated through one of these three causes.

Descartes's list is not an arbitrary concoction. Cicero in his *De fato* lists all three causes. The Stoics maintained, Cicero writes, that the world came into existence through Fate; the Epicureans held that it was chance which brought the world into being; the third alternative, Cicero says, was the invention of "the most moderate" Stoic, Chrysippus, "an honorary arbiter . . . [who] holds a middle course" (chapt. xvii) between those "philosophers who introduce a chain of eternal causes of absolute necessity (*causarum seriem sempiternam*)" (chapt. ix) and "[Epicurus who] thinks that the necessity of fate is avoided by this fortuitousness of atoms" (chapt. x).[34]

34 To my knowledge only Henri Gouhier's *La pensée métaphysique de Descartes* (Paris: Vrin, 1978 ed., p. 120) mentions the Epicureans and Stoics. However, Gouhier confines his discussion to one sentence: "L'ignorance où je suis du principe dont dépendent mon être et mes facultés, cette ignorance présuppose le problème métaphysique de mon orig-

We could try to elaborate on the differences between the respective positions of the Epicureans, the Stoics, and Chrysippus, and speculate on possible reasons that might have made Descartes introduce them in this part of the *Meditations* and take a stance against them.[35] However, the fact that Descartes lumps them together under the label of "some people" (*nonnulli qui*) should be taken as an indication that he probably thought the differences between their respective positions were less relevant than what they had in common.

> ine. A côté des solutions stoïcienne et épicurienne, l'hypothèse d'un Créateur dont la toute-puissance menacerait mes vérités ne serait-elle point conçue à partir du vrai Dieu mais pas encore assez clairment connu?" According to Stefano Di Bella (*Meditazioni metafisiche: Introduzione alla lettura,* [Rome: NIS, 1997], p. 54) the *continuata rerum serie* hypothesis is a reference to Aristotelian theory. However, he does not cite any text to endorse his claim.

35　In responding to my article, Georges Moyal, *op. cit.*, p. 161, dismisses my supposition by saying: "There is thus no reason to think that the people Descartes alludes to, in the passage under scrutiny, are Epicureans or Stoics, or that he intends to respond to their specific variety of atheism: there is no reason to think that the text goes beyond the problem of error. Nor do the *Meditations* hint at what an answer to the argument from evil might look like." First, I nowhere claim that Descartes intends to respond to "their *specific* variety of atheism" (emphasis mine). However, from this it does not follow that Descartes does not have any intention of responding to them as a group. Descartes clearly offers such a response in the same paragraph when he says: "Because to be deceived and to err seem to be certain imperfections, the less powerful an author of my origin *these people* will assign, [etc.]" (emphasis mine). Second, it appears strange to me that Moyal ignores my claim despite the fact that I bring in textual evidence from Cicero (with whose writings Descartes almost certainly was familiar) where the three causes are mentioned. Be that as it may, if I am mistaken in my identification of the three causes, the question arises: (1) why did Descartes bring them in? and (2) what possible purpose did he have in mind in invoking three competing theories of the origin of the world to which ancient thinkers subscribed? Finally, *if* the "text [of the *Meditations*] does not go beyond the problem of error" why did Descartes make the following claim in Meditation IV: "Since the will is indifferent in such cases, it easily turns aside from what is true and good, and this is the source of my error and *sin*" (AT VII, 58; SCM II, 41; emphasis mine). Besides, when Descartes says in the same Meditation, "In this incorrect use of free will may be found the *privation* which constitutes the essence of error," he uses a strictly theological notion, which Augustine invented to explain the origin of evil.

But what could such diverse philosophies have in common? Again, the next sentence provides an explanation: "Because to be deceived and to err seem to be certain imperfections, *the less powerful an author of my origin* these people will assign, the more probable will it be that I am so imperfect that I would always be deceived" (*quo minus potentem originis meae authorem assignabunt, eo probabilius erit me tam imperfectum esse ut semper fallar*). In other words, the respective positions held by the *nonnulli qui*, the differences between them notwithstanding, come down to limiting the power of the source of my being.

In 1647 Descartes was accused of blasphemy by two Leiden theologians for holding the evil genius to be omnipotent. Only God is omnipotent, as they claimed. Descartes firmly rejected the accusation by reiterating the argument from this passage in the First Meditations: to account for deception, Descartes explained defending himself, it is not necessary to assume that the deceiver is all-powerful; it is enough to assume that I originated through a cause less than all-powerful: "good needs a faultless cause while evil follows any defect" (*bonum esse in integra causa, malum autem ex quouis defectu*).[36] One can read this argument in the following way: the reliability of my cognitive apparatus is (directly?) proportional to the power of the original source of my cognitive nature. Because every possible source of my cognitive nature other than God is less than omnipotent, my liability to error can simply be due to the fact that I was not *created* by God but *originated* "by some other means." In other words, the likelihood of my cognitive nature being deceptive increases as the omnipotence of the source of my being decreases.

The introduction of the *nonnulli qui* marks an essential change in Descartes's argument. The earlier entertained hypothesis of the *deus deceptor* implies that mathematics can be rendered dubitable by the all-powerful *ratio dubitandi* (God), while in [2] it is a less than omnipotent First Cause which renders mathematics dubitable. What remains unexplained is the way in which a non-omnipotent source of my nature can render mathematics

---

36 Letter to the Curators of Leiden University, 4 May 1647 (AT V, 8; CSMK III, 316).

dubitable. As I suggested earlier by invoking the distinction between *scientia* and *persvasio* from his *Second Set of Replies*, Descartes's concern there is the kind of knowledge one can have regarding mathematics. And, as he neatly explained to the authors of the *Second Set of Objections*, the unshaken "awareness" of 2 + 3 = 5 is insufficient to call it *scientia*. What is necessary to transform awareness into *scientia* is the knowledge of the existence of God on whom eternal verities depend.

III

Descartes's next step in paragraph [2] aims at exposing the short-comings of the *nonnulli qui's* reasoning. The introductory sentence reads: "But there might perhaps be some people (*nonnulli qui*) who would prefer to deny the existence of a God so powerful (*tam potentem aliquem Deum*) than to believe that all other things (*res alias omnes*) are uncertain." The phrasing is somewhat strange, particularly the expression "God so powerful." If Descartes worked on the traditional conception of God, he would have no need to say "so powerful" (*tam potentem*). Only the Cartesian creator of mathematical verities can render everything else uncertain.

If, as I suggested above, the *deus deceptor* hypothesis rests on the 1630 doctrine, the reaction of the *nonnulli qui* is not a reaction to any traditional conception of God but to Descartes's own conception of God – the God who, unlike any other God, is the author of these truths. Accordingly, if God's power extends to the essences of things, He can freely change them, and by the same token His existence, instead of being the foundation of certitude, becomes the source of the truths' instability. Descartes anticipated and addressed this concern already in 1630, when in his letter to Mersenne, 15 April, he wrote: "It will be said that if God had established these truths He could change them as a king changes his laws." And he adds: "To this the answer is: Yes He can, if His will can change. 'But I understand them to be eternal and unchangeable.' – I make the same judgment about God."

This argument is absent from the *Meditations*. What we find there ([2]) in its stead is the juxtaposition of the omnipotent cause (God) and an "impotent" one (*seu causa . . .*), preceded in the French version with the following sentence: "Let us not oppose

them [the *nonnulli qui*] for a moment and grant them that everything said about God is a fable." The denial of the existence of God
leads to the implicit acceptance of an alternative theory about the
world's origin. There are three such causes (chance, fate, and the
continuous series of causes). None of them, Descartes remarks –
turning the argument of the *nonnulli qui's* against them – is
omnipotent, which means that the likelihood of my having a nature
which goes wrong increases. Descartes repeated the same argument in two other places: in his letter of 4 May 1647 to the
Curators of Leiden University, when he defended himself against
the charges of blasphemy for allegedly implying that the deceiver
is omnipotent, and in his *Sixth Set of Replies*: "As for the knowledge possessed by the atheist, it is easy to demonstrate that it is
not immutable and certain. As I have stated previously, the less
power the atheist attributes to the author of his being, the more
reason he will have to suspect that his nature may be so imperfect
as to allow him to be deceived even in matters which seem utterly
evident to him."[37]

One way to understand Descartes's argument is the following:
omnipotence is an attribute of a *personal* creator. Personality in
turn implies intelligence: only a personal and intelligent creator is
capable of *designing* a nature which would not go wrong;[38] if I owe
my nature to a cause other than God, my nature by definition lacks
a design, and therefore it is *naturally* subject to error.[39]

Descartes's argument leaves room for the following objection. I

---

37 AT VII, 428, CSM II, 289.
38 Cf. Letter to Mesland, 2 May 1644. AT IV, 113; CSMK III, 232.
39 In my reading of the literature on Descartes I did not come across a
coherent explanation of how one should understand Descartes's argument
that the non-omnipotence of the three causes makes my nature even
more susceptible to deception. Most scholars rephrase Descartes's statement. For example, Ferdinand Alquié (*Œuvres philosophiques de
Descartes*, vol. II, p. 410, footnote 1) confines himself to the following
remark: "[M]oins mon auteur sera puissant, plus j'aurai de chances de me
tromper. On peut donc conclure, que Dieu, étant tout-puissant et infini,
ne peut me tromper." Recently this passage was very briefly commented
on by Jean-Marie Beyssade. See his "'Devenir athées.' Sur un passage controversé de la Première Méditation," *Archives de Philosophie* (Bulletin
Cartésien, XX), vol. 55 (1992), pp. 3–6.

have a nature which sometimes goes wrong. If I was created by God I should have a nature which never goes wrong. Descartes defended himself against this objection in the Fourth Meditation by saying that to phrase the problem in this way is to confuse the *individual* man's absolute cognitive infallibility[40] with perfection.[41] To a large extent the whole of the Fourth Meditation is devoted to meeting this objection.

If my suggestion that the *nonnulli qui's* reaction is a response to Descartes's own conception of God is correct, the hypothesis of the *deus deceptor* is connected with the doctrine of the eternal truths that he formulated in his three famous letters to Mersenne in 1630. However, if this is the case, then in the ranks of the *nonnulli qui* we find not only the Epicureans, the Stoics, Chrysippus, atheists, or atheist mathematicians, but virtually all thinkers, including Aquinas, for whom laws of mathematics are binding on God. That is why, I believe, Descartes uses the vague term *nonnulli qui* rather than the term *athei* which had a very definite content in the 17th century Europe. This part of the *Meditations* is, in my opinion, not only a very carefully crafted dialogue between Descartes and the exponents of ancient and 0odern philosophies, but also points to a fundamental weakness of Aquinas's doctrine which failed to secure the link between the dependence of mathematics on God.

40 In Meditation IV (AT VII 61, CSM II, 42) Descartes says very explicitly that God could create human nature in such a way that "I should never make mistakes."

41 "It occurs to me, also, that whenever we inquire as to whether the works of God would be perfect, not some one creature separately, but rather the whole universe of things is to be regarded. For what would perhaps not without merit seem very imperfect if it were alone is, as having the nature of a part in the world, most perfect" (Med. IV, 7); and: "But I cannot therefore deny that in a certain mode it be a greater perfection in the total universe of things that certain ones of its parts were not immune from errors, but other ones were so immune, than if all the parts would be wholly similar" (Med. IV, 15). Cf. Gibieuf, *De Libertate Dei et creatrae*, Paris, 1630, p. 441 (*Videlicet, etsi multa sint. relata ad creaturas et naturas earum, ad providentiam tamen comparata, omnia bona sunt, satem per modum medii, quia omnia ad bonum aliquod conferunt*); St. Augustine, *Enchiridion*, chaps. 11, 95, 96, 99, 100; St. Thomas, *Summa Theologiae*, I, 48, 2 *ad Resp*.

Let me move on to address one final point. If the question of the origin and nature of error can be reduced to the problem of the source of human nature, *who* or *what* then is the evil genius introduced at the end of the First Meditation, which brought on Descartes the wrath of the Protestant theologians in 1647 and made Cartesian scholars believe that the evil genius is an omnipotent deity stripped of his goodness?[42] In the Sixth Meditation, in reviewing the reasons which led him "to doubt so many things in the past few days," Descartes observes: "[S]ince [in the First Meditation] I was still *ignorant of the author of my origin* (or at least was pretending to be ignorant thereof) I saw nothing to rule out the possibility that my natural constitution made me prone to error even in matters which seemed to me most true."[43] This pronouncement leaves little room for the interpretation that the *ratio dubitandi* of mathematics is a *personal* and malicious deity whose omnipotence poses a threat to the "continuity" of our clear and distinct perceptions. The evil genius is the *representation* of the *weakness* of human cognitive nature which originated through a non-omnipotent cause. As Henri Gouhier aptly put it, "the ignorance of the source of my being poses a metaphysical problem: Whence man? Its epistemological formula is the following: Whence reason?" In other words, while the metaphysical question is about the source of human existence – *who* or *what* brought man into existence?: was man *created* (by God) or did he *originate* (through *fato, casu, continuata rerum serie*) – the epistemological question, *whence reason?* concerns the status of the clear and distinct ideas: Are the clear and distinct perceptions – which have their seat in the human mind – merely an expression of the way *my* mind functions, or are they the rules constitutive for every *created creature*?

42 It is worth quoting Geroult's insightful observation here: "[S]ince God's omnipotence is by nature capable of freely instituting truths other than those that have been created, while it is incapable to deceive by its nature, there is no common ground between the theory of eternal truths and the hypothesis of the evil genius." *Ibid.*, p. 22.

43 AT VII, 77; CSMK II, 53. Descartes repeated the same idea in the *Principles of Philosophy* I, 13: "[T]he possession of certain knowledge will not be possible until it [the mind] has come to know the author of its being."

To put it in a different way, what stands behind those two questions, and thus behind Descartes's quest for Certitude, is, as Gouhier put it, "an intellectual inquietitude of the soul tormented by the secret of its origin."[44]

---

44 Henri Gouhier, *La pensée métaphysique de Descartes*, *op. cit.*, p. 120. Cf. pp. 162–75. See also his *Essais sur le "Discours de la méthode," la méthaphysique, et la morale* (Paris: Vrin, 1973), pp. 162–75; "L'ordre des raisons selon Descartes," *Cahiers de Royaumont, Philosophie No II, Descartes*, pp. 72–87, followed by a discussion (pp. 88–108) between Gouhier and Gueroult, Prenant, Perelman, Beck, Alquié, Hypolite, Lefebvre, Boehm, and Hersh.

How to Read Descartes's Second and Sixth Meditations:
On the Aristotelian-Thomistic and Cartesian Soul and Its Union with the Body

Explicit criticism of Aristotle and his Scholastic followers is relatively rare in Descartes's official writings. For example, in the *Meditations*, there are only two such references to Aristotelian philosophy. One of them is an *in passim* remark in Meditation Four: "I consider the customary search for final causes to be totally useless in physics'"[1]; the other one is a lengthy passage in the Second Meditation which begins with the memorable words: "What then did I formerly think I was? A man. But what is a man? Shall I say 'a rational animal'?[2] In his use of the word "formerly" Descartes's signals his departure from the Aristotelian tradition which defined man as a rational animal. However, the problem goes deeper than just a mere definition. The definition of man as "a rational animal" stems directly from Aristotle's conception of the oneness of the intellective, sensitive, and nutritive soul in man. Therefore, in rejecting the Aristotelian definition of man, Descartes, despite his

---

1   AT VII, 55; CSM II, 39. All citations from St. Thomas's *Summa Contra Gentiles*, are to Anton Charles Pegis, Vernon J. Bourke, James Anderson, and Charles J. O'Neil translation (Notre Dame, Ind.: University of Notre Dame Press, 1955–1957. This is abbreviated to *SCG*. All citations from *Summa Theologiae* are to the Blackfriars edition (Cambridge/New York: McGraw-Hill, 1964–). This is abbreviated to *ST*.

2   AT VII, 25–27.

proclamations that the soul is the substantial form of the body,[3] in fact broke the substantial union.

I

The problem of the so-called substantiality of the union between the soul and body, as Aquinas presents it in his *Summa Contra Gentiles*, originated with Plato. According to Plato, the soul is a "prisoner" in the body. This kind of a relationship presupposes that the soul is "united to a body by contact of power"[4] and their union, which is analogous to a pusher (soul) to a thing pushed (body),[5] is accidental, rather than substantial. This observation leads Aquinas to the following point: If the union of the soul with a body is "accidental," then souls must enjoy, as they do in Plato, separate existence prior to their union with bodies. Such a union of souls with bodies can be affected only either by "violence" or by "free choice." If it is affected by "violence," man would be "something unnatural."[6] The "voluntary" union is also problematic. In Plato's theory, the "union with the body places an obstacle in the way of the soul's understanding."[7] The Platonic soul in its union with the body is a "victim of [cognitive] deception."[8] If so, the question arises: Why would souls, which prior to their union with bodies had the "power to contemplate truth in a pure manner," be willing to be united with bodies?[9]

Plato's theory explains that the *end* of the soul is the contemplation of Truth (Ideas); it fails, however, Aquinas argues, to explain what is the *end* of man, as the composite of a soul and its body, and, implicitly, *what* is man.

---

3   See, for example, his Reply to Arnauld, *Fourth Set of Replies*, AT VII, 228ff.; CSM, II, 160ff.

4   *SCG*, II, 56 [10].

5   *SCG*, II, 57 [10].

6   *SCG*, II, 83 [12], [17].

7   *SCG*, II, 83 [27]. And: "In no case, however, does nature unite a thing to that which impedes its operation."

8   *SCG*, II, 83 [17]. And: "Especially according to Platonists, who say that through its union with the body, the soul forgets what it knew before, its power to contemplate truth in a pure manner thus being checked."

9   "Now, if the union of souls to bodies is natural, then, in their creation, souls had a natural desire to be united to bodies." *SCG*, II, 83 [13].

The ultimate end of every thing, moreover, is that which it strives to attain by its operations. But man, by all his proper operations fittingly ordered and rightly directed, strives to attain the contemplation of truth. . . . The end of man, therefore, is to arrive at the contemplation of truth. It is for this purpose that the soul is united to the body, and in this union that man's being consists. Therefore, it is not union with the body that causes the soul to lose the knowledge which it had possessed [as Plato maintains – Z. J.]; on the contrary, the soul is united to the body so that it may acquire knowledge.[10]

And:

The body is the soul's housing, so to speak, and the subject that receives it. This explains why the soul's proper operation, understanding, has its object, namely, the phantasm, in the body, despite the fact that this operation does not depend on the body as though it were effected through the instrumentality of a bodily organ. It follows that, so long as the soul is in the body, it cannot perform that act without a phantasm.

"Things united by contact [of power]," like in Plato, "are not unqualifiedly one."[11] Hence, Aquinas concludes, Plato's man is a

10 *SCG*, II, 83, 28. Aquinas anti-Platonic position can also be found in *ST*, Ia. 84, art. 4 (vol. XII, p. 27): "In this [Plato's] view, however, no satisfactory reason can be given why our soul is united to the body. On the one hand, it cannot be said that the intellectual soul (*anima intellectiva*) is united to the body for the sake of the body, because, first, form is not for the sake of matter, nor, second, is the mover for the thing moved – just the reverse. On the other hand, since the soul's existence does not depend upon the body, the body would seem to be especially necessary for the intellectual soul in its characteristic operation, which is understanding. But if the soul were by nature such that it could receive species through the influence of a certain immaterial principle alone, and not from the senses, it would not need the body to understand. Thus it would be united to the body to no purpose." In *ST*, Ia, 84, art. 3 (vol. XII, p. 21), Aquinas develops this point by saying: "if any of the senses is lacking, knowledge of what is apprehended by the sense is also lacking – for instance, a man born blind can have no acquaintance with colors. This would not be so if the natures of all intelligible objects were naturally innate in the soul."
11 *SCG*, II, 56 [10].

being "by accident" (*per accidens*), as opposed to his and
Aristotle's man who is a "being in itself" (*per se*).[12]

The divide between the Platonists and the Aristotelians comes
down to the difference between the inexplicable Platonic "voluntary"
union of the soul and body and the Aristotelian "natural" union. In its
most schematic form this divide can be presented as follows.

According to the Platonists, (1) souls preexist prior to the
union with the body, (2) the end (*telos*) of the soul is the contemplation of Truth (*Ideas*) independent of the human body, (3) the
union of the soul with the body is a cognitive obstacle, (4) man is
an *ens per accidens* (accidental being).

According to the Aristotelians, (1) souls are born along with the
bodies, (2) the soul does not have an end (*telos*) separate from the
body, (3) the intellective soul is the principle of cognitive operations for which the body, connected to it by means of a phantasm,
is indispensable, (4) the soul's union with the body makes man an
ens per se (natural being).

II

Where is Descartes in this debate? Let me quote a well-known passage from the Sixth Meditation:

> There is nothing that my own nature teaches me more
> vividly than that I have a body, and that when I feel pain
> there is something wrong with the body. . . . Nature also
> teaches me, by these sensations of pain, hunger, thirst and
> so on, that I am not merely present in my body as a sailor
> is present in the ship, but that I am very closely joined and,
> as it were, intermingled with it, so that I and the body form
> a unit. . . . For these sensations of hunger, thirst, pain and
> so on are nothing but confused modes of thinking which
> arise from the union and, as it were, intermingling of the
> mind with the body.[13]

---

12 As an example of the contrary view in Plato, one can quote *Phaedo*, 79c:
"Haven't we also said some time ago that when the soul makes use of the
body to investigate something, be it through hearing or seeing or some
other sense – it is dragged by the body to the things that are never the
same, and the soul itself strays and is confused and dizzy, as if it were
drunk, in so far as it is in contact with that kind of thing?"
13 AT VII, 80–81; CSM, II, 56.

The significance of this passage does not lie in the explanation of *how* the soul and the body are connected, since this passage does not offer any explanation for this, but rather in Descartes's use of the metaphor of the sailor and the ship. The metaphor was supposed to be an illustration of Plato's man, whose soul is represented as a sailor in his ship. Now if the soul is capable of existence without a body (ship), Platonic man lacks the unity that would make him *ens per se*.

Descartes's use of the metaphor is hardly accidental. The metaphor was used by Plato in several dialogues – however, he uses it almost always in a political, not epistemological, context. In fact, only in one passage, in the *Laws*, XII, 961e, the metaphor might be said to be of epistemological significance: "But what in particular is the object envisaged by the blended intelligence and sense which is to be the salvation of a vessel in storm and calm? In this case of the ship, *it is the fusion of the sharp senses of captain and crew alike with the captain's intelligence* that preserves the ship and ship's company together, is it not?" Neither the *Laws*, nor the *Phaedo*, nor the *Republic*, where we find some fragments that might justify the ascribing the metaphor to Plato, were known during the Middle Ages. Only some fragments from the *Timaeus*, and *Alcibiades* were known. In none of them, however, do we find anything that could allow for constructing such an image. There is a passage in Aristotle's *De anima* where the words "sailor" and "ship" do occur, but, again, the metaphor in the form we find it in Descartes is not there.[14] The metaphor was used by Plotinus (*Enneads*, IV, 3, 21) and Gregory of Nyssa, or, rather, Nemesius, the true author of *De natura hominis* (chap. 3). Again, although the words "pilot" and "ship" are there, the point of the metaphor seems not to correspond to how it is used in Descartes. The metaphor in this particular form was most likely invented by

---

14 "From this it indubitably follows that the soul is inseparable from its body, or at any rate that certain parts of it are (if it has parts) – for the actuality of some of them is nothing but the actualities of their bodily parts. Yet some may be separable because they are not the actualities of any body at all. Further, we have no light on the problem whether the soul may not be the actuality of its body in the sense in which the sailor is the actuality of the ship" (*De anima*, I, 413a8–9).

Aquinas.[15] It is used in the *Summa Contra Gentiles* (see esp. II, 57 [2]) and in the *Questio disputata de anima*:

> Plato, however, went further, saying not only that the soul subsisted on its own but that it possessed a complete specific nature of its own. For he thought the whole nature of human beings resided in their souls, defining them not as body-soul composites but as souls using bodies, as though souls inhabited bodies like sailors do ships, or people their clothes. But this is impossible. For clearly the life principle is what gives life to the body. But being alive is existing as a living thing. So the soul is that by which the human body actually exists: in other words, it is the sort of thing a form is. So the human soul is the form of the human body. Further, if the soul inhabited the body like a sailor his ship it would not give the body or its parts their specific nature; yet clearly it does since when it leaves the body the various parts lose the names they first had, or keep them in a different sense; for a dead man's eyes are eyes only in the sense that eyes in a picture or a statue are, and the same goes for other parts of the body. Moreover, if the soul inhabited the body like a sailor his ship the union of body and soul would be accidental, and when death separated them

15 In *SCG*, II, 57 [2] Aquinas writes: "Accordingly, Plato and his followers asserted that the intellectual soul is not united to the body as form to matter, but only as mover to the movable, for Plato said that the soul is in the body as a sailor in a ship. Thus the union of soul and body would only be by contact of power – which we have spoken above. And in [4] he adds: Plato asserted that man is not a being composed of body and soul, but that the soul itself using the body is man; just as Peter is not a thing composed of man and cloths, but a man using cloths."
Here Aquinas makes reference to Plato's *Alcibiades I*, 129e, 130c, the dialogue which was known in the Middle Ages. In his *De motu animalium* (esp. 698b8ff.) Aristotle is concerned with similar problem. It is possible that this work by Aristotle and Plato's *Alcibiades I*, plus Aristotle's short remark in the *De anima* I, 413a8, allowed Aquinas to formulate the metaphor in the form in which Descartes presents it in the *Meditations*.
Giordano Bruno, the authors of the Coimbrian Manual, Pierre Charron, and Mersenne also use this metaphor. For the quotations from these authors, see F. Manzini, "Comme un pilote en son navire," *Bulletin Cartésien*, XXXI, 2003. Cf. also, Augustin Mansion, "L'immortalité de l'âme et de l intellect d'après Aristote," *Revue philosophique de Louvain*, No. 51, 1953, pp. 456–65.

it would not lead to the decomposition of a substance, which it clearly is.[16]

The centrality of the metaphor in Descartes seems to suggest two things. First, he wanted to signal his agreement (even if pretended and verbal) with Aquinas. Second, given the incompatibility of their respective epistemologies, Descartes's use of this metaphor suggests that from the Scholastic thinkers it was Aquinas (but also Aristotle) whom Descartes puts himself in to opposition to. However, even if we grant that Descartes did not propose a version of Platonic epistemology, does it follow that the union between the soul and the body in the Cartesian man is substantial?

The question of the substantiality of the union between the soul and the body is the reversal of the problem as to whether man is the *ens per se* or the *ens per accidens*. Descartes was no doubt acquainted with the Scholastic vocabulary of *ens per se* and *ens per accidens*. In his letter to Regius, Descartes writes:

> [W]henever the occasion arises, in public and in private, you should give out that you believe that a human being is a true *ens per se*, and not an *ens per accidens*, and that the mind is united in a real and substantial manner to the body. You must say that they are united not by position or disposition, as you assert in your last paper – for this too is open to objection and, in my opinion, quite untrue – but by a true mode of union, as everyone agrees, *though nobody explains what this amounts to*, and so you need not do so either. You could do so, however, as I did in my *Metaphysics*, by saying that we perceive that sensations such as pain are not pure thoughts of a mind distinct from a body, but confused perceptions of a mind really united to a body.

And Descartes adds:

> For if an angel were in a human body, he would not have sensations as we do, but would simply *perceive* the motions

16 *Questio disputata de anima* (section "In Reply"), English translation by Timothy McDermott, *World's Classics* (Oxford: Oxford University Press: Oxford, 1993), p. 188.

which are caused by external objects, and in this way would
differ from a real man.[17]

What are we to think of Descartes's explanation? Clearly, Descartes
did not think that the idea of a substantial union of a body and the
mind had any definite content ("nobody explains what this
amounts to"). If so, any explanation (provided that we stick to the
Scholastic vocabulary), including the one that Descartes offers in
the Sixth Meditation ("hunger and pain are not pure thoughts of a
mind distinct from a body, but confused perceptions of a mind really united to a body"), could pass for a demonstration of the substantial union. But even if we leave aside Descartes's use of the
same vocabulary, the example of an angel thrown into a human
body shows the incompatibility between his own position vis-à-vis
that of the Angelic Doctor.

In invoking the example of an angel, Descartes is trying to show
Regius that if an intellectual substance such as mind were to be
joined to a human body in a non-substantial way, man would not
feel pain; he would *perceive* a wounded body. Hence, the suggested conclusion that the union between the body and the (human)
mind is substantial.

Considerable parts of the *Summa Theologica* and the *Summa
Contra Gentiles* are devoted to discussing the difference between
the nature of angelic and human minds.[18] Interestingly enough, in

17 Letter to Regius, January, 1642 (AT III, 493; CSMK, III, 206; emphasis
    mine). A few pages later (AT III, 508; CSMK III, 209), in the same letter,
    Descartes says: "But if a human being is considered in himself as a whole,
    we say of course that he is a single *ens per se*, and not *per accidens*;
    because the union which joins a human body and soul to each other is not
    accidental to a human being, but essential, since a human being without
    it is not a human being. One should note that what Descartes says here
    does not seem to make sense. What makes man being *per se* is not
    whether we consider him <as a whole>, that is, a composite of body and
    soul; the question concerns the structure of this union."

        As I suggest in my *Augustinian-Cartesian Index* (South Bend, Ind.:
    St. Augustine's Press, 2004), p. 110, footnotes 39 and 40, and pp. 168–73,
    the *Summa* that Descartes read is the *Summa Contra Gentiles*. It is very
    likely that Descartes's use of the terms *per se* and *per accidens* comes
    from *Summa Contra Gentiles*, II, 52ff.

18 The final part of the *SCG*, II, 91–101 is devoted to separate substances
    (i.e., angels). In the *Summa Theologica*, he discusses them in: Ia, 106–13

the *Summa Contra Gentiles,* II, 91-101, Aquinas does not employ the term "angels." He uses the term "separate substance." (In the *Summa Theologica,* Aquinas employs the term "angel" throughout.) The choice of terminology is not accidental, however. In the *Summa Contra Gentiles* the discussion of the nature of angels is presented right after Aquinas's considerations concerning the union between human intellective soul (form) and the body. Aquinas's discussion of angels revolves around the question as to whether a form can exist apart from matter, and if so, what is the nature of such forms?

> Forms existing in matter are imperfect acts [of being], since they have not complete being. Hence, there are some forms that are complete beings. Hence, there are some forms that are complete acts, subsisting in themselves and having a complete species.[19] But every form that subsists through itself without matter is an intellectual substance, since, as we have seen [*SCG*, II, 82 – Z.J.], immunity from matter confers intelligible being. Therefore, there are some intellectual substances that are not united to bodies, for every body has matter.[20]

The question arises: what do the angelic form and the human form have in common and in what way are they different? Insofar as the human soul is a form of a certain matter, it is, among other things, a form in the sense of the organization of matter; angels are separate from matter. Therefore, "there are many souls of one species, while it is impossible for many angels to be of one species."[21] Hence the necessity of the hierarchy among angels.[22] On the other

[vols. XIV, XVI]. However, in the *ST*, with a few exceptions, there is little of strictly philosophical interest. On one occasion, however, Ia, 107, 1 [vol. XIV, p. 109], when Aquinas is concerned with angelic speech, he says: "we even refer to the concept of the mind as an inner word. . . . [Nam ipse conceptus mentis interius verbum vocatur . . .] We have to make use of an outward, vocalized communication because of the interference of the body. Hence among the angels there is no place for outward, but only for inward speech."

19   *SCG*, II, 91 [3].
20   *SCG*, II, 91 [5].
21   *ST*, I, Q. 76. Art. 2, *Reply Obj.*1.
22   *SCG*, III, 81.

hand, insofar as a form is also the principle of intellectual operations, it is, like an angel, an intellectual substance; however, its
intellectual capacity is both different and lower than in angels.[23]

The next question concerns the way in which an intellectual
substance which is joined to a body acquires knowledge. The starting point for the acquisition of knowledge by the human intellective soul is an image, a *phantasm*, that the soul acquires through
the senses: "in the present life our intellect has a natural relation
to the natures of material things; thus it understands *nothing*
except by turning to sense images."[24] But to come back to the problem, if we hold that the soul, by its very nature, has to understand
by turning to sense images, then, since the nature of the soul is not
changed by the death of the body, it would seem that the soul, naturally speaking, can understand nothing, for there are no sense
images at hand for it to turn to.[25] Now the acts by which, in the
present life, knowledge is acquired include a turning of the intellect
to sense images found in the sense faculties we have mentioned.[26]

23   "The intellective power of a separate substance [angel] is higher than that
      of a human soul, since, as we have also shown, the intellect with which
      the *human soul is endowed is the lowest in the order of intellects." SCG*,
      II, 96 [3]. Cf. *ST*, Ia, 89, 1 (Reply) [vol. XIV, p. 141]: "Now evidently
      among intellectual substances, in the order of nature, human souls are
      the lowest/Manifestum est autem inter substantias intellectuales, secun-
      dum naturae ordinem, infimas esse animas humanas."

24   "[S]ecundum Aristotelis sententiam, quam magis experimur, intellectus
      noster, secundum statum praesentis vitae, naturalem respectum habet ad
      naturas rerum materialium; unde nihil intellegit nisi convertendo se ad
      phantasmata." *ST*, Ia. 88, 1 (Reply).

25   "Et ideo ad hanc difficultatem tollendam, considerandum est quod, cum
      nihil operetur nisi inquantum est actu, modus operandi uniuscujusque rei
      sequitur modum essendi ipsius. Habet autem anima alium modum essen-
      di cum unitur corpori, et cum fuerit a corpore seperata, manente tamen
      eadem animae natura." *ST*, Ia, 89, 1 (Reply).

26   And: *ST*, Ia, 84, 7 (Reply): "It is impossible for our intellect, in its present
      state of being joined to a body capable of receiving impressions, actually
      to understand anything without turning to sense images/Dicendum quod
      impossibile est intellectum nostrum, secundum praesentis vitae statum
      quo possibili corpori conjugitur, aliquid intelligere in actu, nisi conver-
      tendo se ad phantasmata."

      "Now it has already been mentioned that while the soul is joined to
      the body it understands by turning to sense images/Dictum est autem

Thus through these acts, there is, on the one hand, in the possible intellect, a certain ability acquired for considering things received through the species and, on the other hand, in the lower faculties alluded to, a certain aptitude acquired for seconding the intellect, so that it can see intelligible objects more easily by turning to them.[27]

> quod quamdiu anima corpori est unita, intelligit convertendo se ad phantasmata." *ST*, Ia. 89, 2 (Reply).
>
> *ST*, Ia. 89, 6 (2; cf. Reply): "But we cannot understand now through species except by turning to sense images, as we have stated/Sed per species intelligibiles non possumus modo intelligere, nisi convertendo nos super phantasmata, sicut supra habitum est."

27 Aquinas' difficulty is the opposite to that of Descartes. The starting point of Descartes's philosophy boils down to finding a way to "detach the mind from the senses" (*abducere mentem a sensibus*) in order to acquire the knowledge of the soul and God. According to Aquinas, a withdrawal of the mind from the senses in the present life would lead to ecstasy: "And this is all the more true of those in a fainting condition or in ecstasy, since such states involve an even greater withdrawal from the bodily senses. . . . Now, the final limit to which contemplation can reach is the divine substance. Hence, the mind which sees the divine substance must be completely cut off from the bodily senses, either by death or by ecstasy" (*SCG*, II, 81–82 [12], III, 47 [2]). And Aquinas adds: "Thus, it is said by one who speaks for God: Man shall not see me and live" (Exod. 33:20).

However, there is some ambiguity in Aquinas on this point. For example, in *SCG* 81–82 [12] he writes: "For the more the soul is freed from the preoccupation with its body, the more fit it becomes for understanding higher things. Hence, the virtue of temperance, which withdraws the soul from bodily pleasures, is especially fruitful in making men apt in understanding."

One can pose two questions, which I am not going to delve into here. Descartes deliberately chose meditations as a form of his philosophical enterprise. (See my *Augustinian-Cartesian Index*, pp. 101–2, where I briefly allude to this problem. See also the bibliographical references on this subject included there.) First, how did he imagine the detachment from the senses without falling into ecstasy? Second, if, as Aquinas says, the knowledge of God's essence is accessible only through ecstatic (or mystical) experience or death, Descartes's project of detaching the mind from the senses should override the limitations of Scholastic philosophy. Aquinas, on the other hand, describes the human soul as situated on the boundary line between corporeal and incorporeal substances, as though it existed on the horizon of eternity and time, [thus approaching] the highest by withdrawing from the lowest. *SCG*, II, 80–81 [12]. Cf. II, 68 [6].

An act of understanding of the species abstracted from a phantasm is, however, an operation that is *not* exercised through a corporeal organ, such as the sense of sight or touch.[28] Understanding is an act of the intellect or of the intellective soul.[29] In this sense, the intellect is independent of the body; however, it is connected to it through sensory perception. At this point, one would like to know whether the fact that the intellective soul, as Aristotle himself argues, is separable from the body,[30] is immortal. There are, it seems, two separate arguments in Aquinas. In the first one, which I am not going to analyze here, but only allude to, Aquinas argues for the substantiality of the soul, that is to say, the soul is a separate substance. However, even if it is, the question arises, how can the intellective soul still operate on the cognitive level if the death of the body severs the influx of phantasms?[31] Aquinas does not offer an argument here. He solved this problem by seeking recourse to Divine intervention. In the *Summa Theologica* Aquinas writes:

> The abstraction of species from sensible objects is done by means of the external senses and other sense faculties, and none of these retain their actuality in the separated soul. Instead, the separated soul *understands singulars* by the infusion of species from the divine light . . .[32]

28 "Actus autem intellectus ex quibus in praesenti vita scientia acquiritur, sunt per conversionem intellectus ad phantasmata, quae sunt in praedictis viribus sensitivis. Unde per tales actus et ipsi intellectui possibili acquirtur facultas quaedam ad considerandum per species susceptas; et in praedictis inferioribus viribus acquiritur qaedam habilitas ut facilius per conversionem ad ipsas intellectus possit intelligibilia speculari." Ia. 89, 5 (*Reply*).

29 *SCG*, II, [8]; cf. 90 [4].

30 *De anima*, III, 429b4: the faculty of sensation is dependent upon the body; mind is separable from it. For St. Thomas's reading of this passage, see his *Commentary on Aristotle's De anima*, Lecture VII, p. 699 (Intellectual Abstraction), translated by Kenelm Foster and Silvester Humphries (Notre Dame, Ind.: Dumb Ox Books, 1994), p. 210.

31 Interestingly enough, Aquinas does not discuss this question in *SCG*, II, as one would expect him to. He merely confines himself to remarking that "after separation from the body, the soul will understand in a different way." See *SCG*, II, 80–81 [10]. He discusses this question extensively in *ST*, Ia, 89, 1–8.

32 "abstractio specierum a sensibus fit mediantibus sensibus et aliis potentiis sensitivis, quae in anima seperata actu non manent. Intelligit autem

The reason for introducing Divine intervention is not, as it might appear, Aquinas's inability to formulate a coherent argument that would make it possible for a separate substance operate without a body; Aquinas formulated such an argument when he argued for the angelic cognition of singulars. Rather, if the human intellect or the intellective soul is incapable of operating on its own after the death of its body, it is because, unlike angels, it was *not* created as a separate form or substance.[33] "The human soul was created as an act of being and the (intellectual) form of a body."[34] However, insofar as only one species of animals – man – is capable of understanding, the intellective soul, thanks to Divine intervention, has the capacity to function without the body of which it was an intellective form/soul when they were joined together.

Aquinas differentiates here between several grades of existence, and several forms of intellects, of which human intellect is the lowest.[35] Existence or, what amounts to the same thing, form as an act of being, without bodies is natural *only* in the case of separate substances (angels); however, it is an *accidental* competence on the part of souls, since that which is through itself (man, who is composed of body and the act of existence or form, for example) must be prior to that which is by accident (that is, man's intellective soul living a separate existence after the body's death[36]). In *Questio disputata de anima*, Aquinas says: "the [soul] is

anima seperata singularia per influxum specierum ex divino lumine, quod quidem lumen . . ." Ia. 89, 7 (Reply), p. 159. And: "The separated souls will get their knowledge under the influence of divine light"/"animae seperatae habebunt scientiam per influentiam divini luminis." Ia. 89, 5.

33 In *ST*, Ia, 89, 1 (Reply), vol. XII, pp. 141–42, Aquinas adds that the perfection of the universe demanded that human souls be joined to bodies so that they could "receive proper knowledge of sensible things from things themselves."

34 "Body and soul are not two actually existing substances; rather, the two of them constitute one actually existing substance. For man's body is not actually the same while the soul is present and when it is absent; but the soul makes it actually." *SCG*, II, 69 [2].

35 *SCG*, II, 45 [3]. *ST*, Ia, 89, 1 (Reply) [vol. XIV, p. 141]: "Now evidently among intellectual substances, in the order of nature, human souls are the lowest"/"Manifestum est autem inter substantias intellectuales, secundum naturae ordinem, infimas esse animas humanas."

36 *SCG*, II, 91.

something which *completes* a human being's specific nature by
being the form of a human body. So that the soul is at one and the
same time a form and itself a thing."[37] And he adds:

> If soul is body's form, body and soul must share one exis-
> tence in common, the existence of the thing [man] they
> compose. . . . What decomposes [after death], properly
> speaking, is neither form nor matter nor existence, but the
> composite of formed matter, the thing. We talk of body hav-
> ing a decomposable existence inasmuch as body through
> decomposition loses the existence it shared in common with
> soul, an existence which remains in the subsistent soul.[38]

What Aquinas is saying is this: if human souls were in fact capable
of existing by themselves, they would not need bodies; they would
be separate substances, like angels, who were not created prior to
bodies in order to enter them. Hence the need for Divine intervention after death. Therefore, if human souls were separate substances which were somehow joined to bodies, then man would not
be man *per se* but *per accidens* because his act of being would pre-
cede the creation of his body.

One might ask the following question: wouldn't the Platonic *per
accidens* position be easier in the context of the Christian premise
that the natural place of the soul (the soul in the religious sense,
that is, that which survives the body) is in heaven, and its union
with the body is only temporary? The simplest answer would be
the following: Aquinas's conception is a continuation of Aristotle's
conception of the soul, and he merely developed it in the direction
Aristotle's conception pointed to. This is not entirely satisfactory,
however. First, within the context of the Christian theological tradition, a version of Platonism was advanced, for example, by
Origen. According to Origen's teaching, souls were created as separate substances. After the Fall, they were joined to bodies.
Depending on the gravity of the sin, some were joined to bodies of
plants (the lowest rank), animals (a higher rank), and yet others to
human bodies (the highest rank).[39] In Origen's account, Aquinas
remarks, the production of man is a matter of chance, from which

37 *Questio De anima, op. cit.,* p. 198.
38 *Questio De anima,* Answers to #13 and #14, *ibid.,* p. 191.
39 Origen, *Peri Archon,* I, 6 (PG, 11, col. 170).

it follows that the union between the soul and its body is accidental[40] and his man is *ens per accidens*. This doctrine was condemned in 553 A.D. by the Council of Constantinople. In the
Orthodox Christian teaching,[41] the human mind or soul is not a
separate substance; it was not created independent of a body, nor
did it preexist to enter it, like the Platonic soul; nor, what is most
important, will the human soul become like an angel after the
death of its body.[42] Therefore a union of an angel and a (human)
body is precluded *ex definitione*.

Second, in his *Commentary on St. Paul's First Letter to the
Corinthians*, 15: 17–19, Aquinas states: "Firstly, if we deny the res-
urrection of the body it is not easy – indeed it becomes very difficult – to defend the immortality of the soul. The union of body and
soul is certainly a natural one, and any separation of soul from
body goes against its nature and is imposed on it. So if a soul is
deprived of its body it will exist imperfectly as long as that situation lasts." However, as Aquinas makes clear on a number of occasions, the human soul does *not* possess a complete specific nature
of its own; rather, it is something which *completes* a human being's
specific nature by being the form of a human body.

From Aquinas's perspective Descartes is clearly mistaken in
thinking that an angel could inhabit a human body. One can of
course argue that he merely gave Regius this example to illustrate
the impossibility of such a union. At the same time, the example
was supposed to demonstrate that if the union between an intellectual substance (mind) and a body were not substantial, the
Cartesian man would not feel pain. However, from the fact the
Cartesian man feels pain,[43] it does not follow at all that the union

40 *SCG*, III, 83 [23].
41 Aquinas briefly discusses the heretical position of Origen in *SCG*, II, 83
    [12], [21–22], 91 [10] and that of Apuleius and certain Platonists in 90
    [13].
42 "The reason why the human soul is not going to become like an angel is
    that even though it is, like an angel, a form, unlike angels, who were cre-
    ated without matter, human form was created to join and individuate mat-
    ter, whereas angels have their principle of individuation in the forms
    itself." *ST*, I, Q. 76. Art. 2, *Reply Obj*.
43 An example that would work better to demonstrate Descartes point
    (unfortunately not available to him) would be a patient under the influ-

is substantial; all that follows is that the Cartesian man, like the Platonic man *per accidens*, feels pain.

III

Let me approach the same question of the alleged substantiality of the union between the soul and the body of the Cartesian man from a different angle. In the two complementary discussions in the *Summa Theologica*, I, Q. 76. Art. 3 and in the *Summa Contra Gentiles*, II, 91 [3], Aquinas considers the question of the substantial union from the point of view of what it means for a man to be a rational animal. In the *Summa Theologica* Aquinas begins his discussion by invoking, again, Plato's view, according to which man has several souls, each of which is responsible for different functions. This view, Aquinas claims, could be maintained only *if* the soul were united to a body as its mover, but not as its form. The Aristotelian-Thomistic view requires that "a rational animal" have *one* soul, not three: vegetative, by which one would be living; sensitive, by which one would be an animal, and intellectual by which one would be man.[44] Otherwise he would not be absolutely one. The oneness of man is guaranteed by one and only one form, by which (1) he has being (*nihil enim est simpliciter unum nisi per formam unam, per quam habet res esse*), is (2) an animal, and (3) is rational. Thus a biped is not distinct from an animal; were a biped distinct from an animal, he would not be absolutely one.[45] Likewise, the form of man, who is both rational and an animal, must have one form.

The second argument is based on the relationship between predicates and forms. Things that are derived from various forms are predicated on one another *accidentally* or *essentially*. An example of accidental predication is the following: "something white is sweet." Whiteness is not necessarily part of being sweet. In

ence of anesthesia. Such a person could indeed *perceive* a wound, say, in his leg or arm or any other part of his body, without *feeling* pain. The state of anesthesia that extends throughout one's body would be a situation where the union of the soul and body would demonstrate lack of connection between one's intellect and one's body.

44 Aristotle discusses this question (criticizing Plato) in his *Metaphysics*, Book H (VIII), 1043b10ff, and 1045a10–19.

45 Cf. Aristotle, *Metaphysics*, VII, 6, 1045a14.

this case forms are not ordered one to another. In essential predication, forms are ordered one to another, that is, when the subject is contained in the definition of a predicate. An example of an "essential predication" is: rational animal (man is contained in the predicate rational). Animal is predicated of man essentially, not accidentally. Therefore, Aquinas concludes, "it is by the same form that a thing is animal and man" (*Ergo oportet eamdem formam esse per quam aliquid est animal, ut sic animal per se de homine praedicatur*), which entails that the nutritive soul, the sensitive soul, and the intellective soul are in man numerically one and the same soul."

In the *Summa Contra Gentiles*, II, 91 [3], Aquinas argues in a similar fashion: Everything included in the essence of the genus (rational) must be found in that of the species (animal). Thus rational belongs to the essence of man, but not to the essence of animal.

In Descartes's letter to Regius, we find the following statement:

> There is only one soul in human beings, the *rational soul*: for no actions can be reckoned human unless they depend on reason. The *vegetative power* and the *power of moving the body*, which are called the *vegetative* and *sensory souls* in plants and animals, exist also in human beings; *but in the case of human beings they should not be called souls,* because they are not the first principle of their actions, and they belong to a totally different genus from the rational soul. . . . And since the mind, or *rational soul*, is distinct from the body, &c., it is with good reason that it *alone* is called the *soul*.[46]

Aquinas would agree with Descartes that "not every principle of vital action is a soul," for, as he says, "then the eye would be a soul, as it is a principle of vision; and the same might be applied to other instruments of the soul.[47] But it is the *first principle of life* which we call the soul." However, in contradistinction to Descartes, in Aristotle and Aquinas operations pertaining to bodily functions, be

46 Letter to Regius, May 1641. AT, III, 371; CSMK III, 182.
47 *ST*, I, 75, Art. 1 (Answer). Emphasis mine. Note that Descartes's wording from his letter to Regius is very similar to that of Aquinas, and it is probable that Descartes read this part of *Summa Theologica*.

it vegetation or movement, stem from the vegetative and sensitive powers or capacities of the same rational soul.

One of the problems with Descartes's explanation is the following: if no action can be called human unless it proceeds from reason, one could say that no action pertaining to the human body, such as walking or eating, should be called human, even though it is a man who eats and walks, or, my eating or walking is human only when I *consciously* decide that I want to walk or eat. This is rather a strange definition of what a human action is. However, it is consistent with Descartes's definition of the *ego* which comprises only mental acts. Secondly, contrary to what Descartes claims, vegetative and moving powers are not souls in man (even though they are souls in animals or plants); they are powers of a soul. Besides, those powers do not belong to a different genus in the case of man, as Aquinas maintains in his discussion concerning essential predication. What belongs to plants (nutritive soul) and to animals (sensitive soul), also belongs to man in virtue of the *oneness* of the soul.

The fragment from the letter to Regius is, I believe, hardly an interpretative error on Descartes's part, and the choice of vocabulary seems intentional. Had Descartes defined the soul, as does Aquinas, as "the principle of life," rather than "the principle of action," he would have to answer the question: *whose* life is the soul a principle of? Man's life? But (the Aristotelian-Thomistic) man is not just the mind or soul but the composite of soul and body. Therefore, in the Second Meditation Descartes, when he suspended the existence of bodies, was at the same time forced to dismiss the Aristotelian definition of man as a rational animal, and all that the structure of the Aristotelian man requires:

> What then did I formerly think I was? A man. But what is a man? Shall I say a rational animal? No; for then I should have to inquire what an animal is, what rationality is, and in this way one question would lead me down the slope to other harder ones, and I do not now have the time to waste on subtleties of this kind.[48]

In rejecting the Aristotelian definition of man, Descartes frees the operations of the mind from the dependence on the image – which

48 Second Meditation, AT VII, 25; CSMK II, 17.

is the cornerstone of Aristotelian epistemology – and thus on the union with a body. Provided that the rational soul can operate in an image-free vacuum, can it still be a form of the body and, thus, can the union of such a soul with a body be substantial?

> For one thing to be another's substantial form, two require-ments must be met. First, the form must be the principle of the substantial being of the thing of whose form it is; I speak not of the productive but of the formal principle whereby a thing exists and is called a being. The second requirement then follows from this, namely, that the form and the mat-ter be joined together in the unity of one act of being; which is not true of the union of the efficient cause with that to which it gives being. And the single act of being is that in which the composite substance subsists: a thing one in being and made up of matter and form.[49]

One would look in vain for a more eloquent definition of the substantial union in Aquinas. First, there is nothing in the notion of the Cartesian rational soul, as defined by the attributes of the *ego* (thought, judgment, will, etc.), that would require it to have a body (which in Aristotle is indispensable for acquiring images); in the Cartesian scheme, my body can be said to be human in virtue of my having it;[50] however, any other body (e.g., of an ass) joined to a rational soul, would also be human. Secondly, Aquinas's first point above requires that the soul be the *act of being* of the whole thing.[51] Again, the Cartesian soul, insofar as it can be called an act of being, is an act of being of that which is not bodily, and there-fore, it would be more appropriate to call it an act of being of itself rather than the *anima* of (biological) life. But what would such an act of being of itself be like?

49   *SCG*, II, 68 [3].
50   In my *Cartesian Theodicy* (Kluwer: Dortrecht/Boston, 2000), I discuss this point in connection with the Doctrine of the Eternal Truths. At the time of writing the *Cartesian Theodicy*, I did not think about this prob-lem. However, it is likely that Aquinas's question as to whether God could create a man who would be an ass comes from Apuleius *Metamorphoses*, to which Aquinas makes references (*SCG*, II, 90 [13]) in connection with the heretical teaching of Origen, who thought that the soul can be joined to a body in a non-substantial way.
51   *SCG*, II, 69 [2].

Ever since the publication of Gilbert Ryle's *The Concept of Mind*, contemporary philosophers of analytic provenance analyze the concept of the Cartesian mind in terms of what they call mental acts. Insofar as the *ego* is about the content of the mind, this line of interpretation is certainly correct. However, it is very restrictive and, from the perspective of the Aristotelian-Scholastic philosophy, to which Cartesianism was a reaction, is anti-metaphysical.

The meaning of the Aristotelian soul, mind, or *anima* is certainly broader than the Cartesian mind. The Aristotelian soul, as Richard Sorabji emphasizes,[52] manifests life, including consciousness in the case of man, whereas in Descartes, it manifests mere consciousness.[53] In Aristotle the statement closest to Descartes's description of the *ego* as consciousness is the following sentence: "the mind too is then able to think itself. . . . Mind itself is thinkable in exactly the same way as its objects are. For in the case of objects which involve no matter, what thinks and what is thought are identical."[54] But if the only feature of the Cartesian *cogito* is consciousness, what is responsible for its being? or is it being itself?

One of Aquinas's fundamental questions concerns the way in which an intellect knows itself or its essence. Aquinas begins by introducing the Aristotelian distinction between two faculties in the intellectual soul: possible and agent intellects. The function of the agent intellect is to abstract species from sensible matter; the

52   Richard Sorabji, "Body and Soul in Aristotle," in *Aristotle's De anima* in focus, ed. by Michael Durrant (London & New York: Routledge, 1993) p. 167. One should read this article in conjunction with Sorabji's *Aristotle on Memory* (Providence, R.I.: Brown University Press, 1972).

53   According to Charles Kahn (see his "Sensation and Consciousness in Aristotle's Psychology," *Archiv für Geschichte der Philosophie*, 48 (1966), pp. 43–81 (reprinted in *Articles on Aristotle*, vol. 4), writes Sorabji, *Ibid.*, pp. 165–167, Aristotle does not have a corresponding word to Cartesian *cogitatio*. "The nearest word [for a mental act in Aristotle] is *aisthanesthia* (perceiving). . . . Nonetheless, as Kahn carefully points out, the word does not correspond to Descartes's *cogitatio*, for Aristotle draws a sharp distinction between thinking and perceiving. He never suggests that thinking is a kind of *aisthanestia*." *Ibid.*, pp. 165–66. I am greatly indebted to Sorabji's article.

54   *De anima*, III, 429b–9; 430a3–5.

function of the possible intellect is to receive the species from already abstracted images.⁵⁵ In this way, the intellect comes from the state of potentiality to actuality. Next Aquinas goes on to contrast the three kinds of intellect: Divine, angelic, and human. The difference between them is the following.

1) The divine intellect is identical with its act of understanding. "Thus for God to understand his own understanding is the same thing as to understand his own essence, for his essence is his understanding."⁵⁶

2) The angelic intellect is not identical with its understanding, even though the primary object of its understanding is its own essence.⁵⁷

---

55 *ST*, Ia, 85, 1, 4, vol., XII, p. 53, and Ia, 84, 6, p. 37, and Ia, 84, 5 [3], p. 29.

56 "Est enim aliquis intellectus, scilicet divinus, qui est ipsum suum intelligere. Et sic in Deo idem est quot intelligat se intelligere, et quod intelligat suam essentiam: quia sua essentia est suum intelligere." *ST*, Ia, 87, 73, *Reply* 1, vol. XII, p. 115. Cf. *SCG*, I, 54 [4], and: "In God the absolute fullness of intellectual knowledge is all contained in one object, namely the unity of the divine essence in which God knows all things. And of this intellectual plenitude created intelligences can have some share, but in a less perfect and less unified way: thus what God knows in and through one medium, all smaller intelligences know in and through many; and the smaller they are the more media they require." "In Deo autem tota plenitudo intellectualis cognitionis continetur in uno, scilicet in essentia divina, per quam Deus omnia cogniscit. Quae quidem intelligibilis plenitudo in intellectibus creatis infriori modo, et minus simpliciter invenitur. Unde oportet quod ea quae Deus cogniscit per unum, inferiores intellectus cognoscant per multa; et tanto amplius intellectus inferior fuerit." *ST*, Ia. 55, 3, Reply, vol. IX, p.105. Cf. Duns, Scotus's *De primo principio*, 4.53.

57 "In angels the action of understanding differs from the act of existing; indeed every action of created beings, whether angels or anything else, is distinct from the act of existing. Therefore an angel's essence is not identical with his power to understand; nor is any created essence identical with a capacity for activity."/"In angelo autem non est idem intelligere et esse; nec aliqua alia operatio aut in ipso, aut quocumque alio creato, est idem quod ejus esse. Unde essentia angeli non est ejus potentia intellectiva, nec aicujus creati essentia est ejus operativa potentia." *ST*, Ia. 54, 3, Reply, vol. IX, p. 83. And: "The essence of an angel is coterminous with the limits of his existence, but not with the full range of his understanding; for not all that an angel understands does he understand through his essence./Ad secundum dicendum quod ipsa essentia angeli est ratio totius

3) "Human intellect is not identical with its understanding nor its own essence, for the primary object of its understanding is something external, namely, the nature of material things. . . ."[58] "The object of the intellect is something general, namely being real and being true. . . . the intellect can understand its own act – but not primarily. For the primary object of our intellect in its present state is not just any being or truth, but the being and truth found in material things, as mentioned, and it comes to a knowledge of all else from these." "One can also note that the reason why human intellect does not know its essence directly is because if it knew, its union with the body, which provides images, would be inexplicable."[59]

ejus esse, non autem est ratio totius ejus intelligere, quia non omnia intelligere potest per suam essentiam." *ST*, Ia, 54, 3 [2], vol. IX, p. 81. "To say, moreover, that in non-material beings intellect is one with its object is the same as to say that, where intellect is in act, this act is also the actuality of what it understands: for what makes a thing to be actually understood is non-materiality. . . . God contains all things as a whole and also even in respect of what is distinctive in each thing; and this is because he is the primary and universal power from which the entirety of each thing proceeds, both what it has in common with other things and what it has proper to itself. God, then, through his essence has a distinct knowledge of all things; but an angel, through his, only a general sort of knowledge."/"Idem est autem quod dicitur, *In his quae sunt sine materia, idem est intellectus et quod intelligitur*; ac si diceretur quod intellectus in actu est intellectum in actu. Ex hoc enim aliquid est intellectum in actu quod est immateriale. . . . In essentia autem Dei sunt omnia perfecte et secundum propriam rationem, sicut in prima et universali virtute operativa, a qua procedit quidquid est in quacumque re vel proprium, vel commune. Et ideo Deus per essentiam suam habet propriam cognitionem de rebus omnibus; non autem angelus, sed solam communem." *ST*, Ia. 55, 2, [2] and [3], vol. IX, p. 97.

58 "et ideo id quod primo cogniscitur ab intellectu humano est hujusmodi objectum; et secundario cognoscitur objectum; et per actum cognoscitur ipse intellectus, cujus est perfectio ipsum intelligere." *ST*, Ia, 87, 73, *Reply* 1, vol. xii, p. 115.

59 "If the soul were by nature such that it could receive the species through the influence of a certain immaterial principle alone, and not from the senses, it would not need the body to understand. Thus it would be united to the body to no purpose / Si autem anima species intelligibiles secundum suam naturam apta nata esset recipire per influentiam aliquorum seperatorum principiorum tantum, et non acciperet eas ex sensibus, non

The above discussion (especially the third point concerning human intellect) in the *Summa Theologica* can be supplemented with Aquinas's considerations from the *Summa Contra Gentiles*, II. In Chapter 60 [4] Aquinas states: Man owes his essence and his human nature to . . . the possible intellect.[60] This argument is aimed against Averroes's view according to which the passive intellect moves the body. However, as Aquinas notices, passive intellect, which is man's ability to understand, is concerned with particulars, "whereas, actual movement involves both the universal judgment, which belongs to the possible intellect, and the particular judgment, which can belong to the passive intellect."[61] Now, possible intellect is cognizant of all sensible forms, as opposed to separate forms; however, reaching to those universal forms is the function of the will, and will can reach only to what the intellect understands. Next, Aquinas points out, universal species are not in passive intellect, "since it is a power using an organ."[62] The agent intellect activates, as it were, possible intellect by sending it phantasms.[63] Aquinas, following Aristotle's lead, according to which mind is nothing before it thinks, makes it more than clear that human intellect can neither know nor exist without bodies from which phantasms are extracted by the agent intellect. "If the possible intellect had *being* separate from body, it would know substances that are separate from matter, rather than sensible forms."[64] Hence Aquinas concludes that "ability to understand is a consequence of the specific nature of man, for understanding is an operation of man as man."[65] Let me emphasize this point, when Aquinas says "man as man," he also means body,[66] without which the intellect would remain, as Aristotle says, nothing.

indigeret corpore ad intelligendum; unde frustra corpori uniretur." *ST*, Ia. 84, 4, vol. XII, p. 27.

60 Cf. *Ibid.*, 62 [13], and *De anima*, III, 429a10.
61 Cf. Aristotle, *De anima*, III, 434a17, and the *Nicomachean Ethics*, VII, 1147a1.
62 *SCG*, II, 60 [13].
63 *SCG*, II, 60 [19] and [14].
64 *SCG*, II, 60 [18].
65 *SCG*, II, 60 [9].
66 "The operation of the possible intellect requires the body, for Aristotle says in the *De anima* II [see 429a15–Z.J.] that the intellect can act by

Now, of all the three intellects – Divine, angelic, and human – the Cartesian mind is like the Divine intellect in that it, first, does not require any medium to begin to be[67]; second, it knows its own essence directly. In contradistinction to the Aristotelian mind, neither does it require bodily organs, through which the agent intellect furnishes an image to the potential intellect to activate it, nor does it need universal forms, as do the angels. Since no phantasm is necessary for the agent intellect to move the potential intellect, the Cartesian mind does not "traverse," as does its Thomistic counterpart, the distance from potentiality to actuality[68]; nor, again, is it divided between the agent and potential intellects. The Cartesian mind is always actual in the same way the Divine mind is. The Cartesian *ego* is first and foremost an act (or intuition) of existence, prior to any conscious mental act, and does not need a body (and therefore the external world) *to be*.

However, if the Cartesian *ego* is an act of being, but not an act of being of the body, like the Aristotelian-Thomistic *anima*, the question arises as to what animates the body of the Cartesian man? Before providing an answer, I would like to turn briefly to Descartes's considerations of the nature of the *ego*, to which the rejection of the Aristotelian definition of man was only a prelude.

Having dismissed the definition of man as a rational animal, Descartes moves on to list the functions which the soul was traditionally responsible for. "Nutrition and movement? Since now I do not have a body, this surely does not occur without a body, these are mere fabrications. Sense perceptions? This surely does not

itself, namely, it can understand when it has been actuated by species abstracted from phantasms – which have no existence apart from body. Therefore, the possible intellect is not altogether separate from body." *SCG*, II, 60 [16].

67 This does not mean that it does not require God to bring it into being.

68 "Mind is in a sense *potentially* whatever is thinkable, though *actually* it is nothing until it has thought. What it thinks must be in it just as characters may be said to be on a writing-tablet on which as yet nothing actually stands written: this is exactly what happens with mind." *De anima*, III, 429b29–30, 430a1–2. Cf. 429a24: "before it [mind] thinks, [it is] not actually any real thing"; 429a22–23: "it follows that it [mind] too, like the sensitive part, can have no nature of its own, than that of having certain capacity."

occur without a body . . ."[69] Having disposed of all the functions or capacities that the Aristotelian soul needs to keep the body alive, Descartes raises the following question:

> But what then am I? A thing that thinks. What is that? A thing that (1) doubts, (2) understands, (3) affirms, (4) denies, is (5) willing, is unwilling, and also (6) imagines and has (7) sensory perceptions.[70]

What is the Aristotelian ego?

> "by mind [*nous*]," Aristotle writes, "I mean that whereby the soul thinks and judges[71] ("judgment involves assertion and denial"[72]) but also imagines[73]; the latter is impossible without sensation.[74]

69   AT VII, 27; CSM II, 18.
70   AT VII, 28, CSM, II, 19. The list of the dismissed attributes of the soul – nutrition, movement (there are two distinctive peculiarities by reference to which we characterize the soul – (1) local movement and (2) thinking, discriminating, and perceiving; thinking, both speculative and practical, is regarded as akin to a form of perceiving. [*De anima*, III, 426a16–19]; see also *De anima*, II, 415b9–11; III, 427a16–18; I, 403b8–9; III 432a4ff.), and sense-perception – corresponds exactly to the functions of the Aristotelian soul in the *De anima*.
71   *De anima*, III, 429a23. And he continues in the same sentence: "For this reason it cannot reasonably be regarded as blended with the body. . . . It was a good idea to call the soul 'the place of forms,' though (1) this description holds only of the intellective soul, and (2) even this is the forms only potentially, not actually" (429a23–29).
72   "To the thinking soul images serve as if they were contents of perception (and when it asserts or denies them to be good or bad it avoids or pursues them). That is why the soul never thinks without an image. . . . The faculty of thinking then thinks the forms in the images . . ." (*De anima*, III, 431a14–17; 431b3). And: Imagination is different from assertion and denial; for what is true or false involves a synthesis of concepts (*Ibid.*, 432a9).
73   427b28–428a12: "Thinking is different from perceiving and is held to be in part imagination, in part judgments: we must therefore first mark off the sphere of imagination and speak of judgment. If then imagination is that in virtue of which an image arises for us . . . is it a single faculty or disposition relative to images, in virtue of which we discriminate and are either in error or not?. . . That imagination is not sense is clear from the following considerations: (1) Sense is either faculty or an activity, e.g., sight or seeing: imagination takes place in the absence of both, as e.g., in dreams. (2) Again, sense is always present, imagination is not . . . (3)

On several occasions, Aristotle even sounds as if he even allowed for the possibility of the "real distinction" between the mind and the body, as, for example, in the following sentence: "The faculty of sensation is dependent upon the body, mind is separable from it."[75] With the exception of the specifically Latin *voluntas*, faculty of the will (however, even this is arguable[76]), the nature of the Aristotelian mind does not, at least at first glance, seem to be different from its Cartesian counterpart. If so, where does the difference between Aristotelian-Thomistic soul and Cartesian soul lie?

"The soul [nous] never thinks without an image" is the Aristotelian epistemological axiom. (Hence the corollary: there is nothing in the intellect that was not previously in the senses.) One may point out, however, that in the Second Meditation Descartes states that (1) imagination and (2) sensory perceptions belong to the *ego*. This is certainly true; however, if one looks closely at how Descartes characterizes the *ego* in this passage, one notices that both sensory perceptions and imagination are included in the *ego* as if only conditionally, only after the emphatic "quoque/and also." The reason for this conditional inclusion, or, should one say, suspension of imagination and sensory perception, is easily explicable. *If* I do not have a body,[77] I cannot perceive, nor can I imagine. The most logical thing would be to read this passage from the Second Meditation in conjunction with Descartes's considerations at the beginning of the Sixth Meditation, when he returns to the subject of sensory perceptions and imagination. There Descartes explains

> Again, sensations are always true, imaginations are for the most part false."

74   "Imagination is held to be a movement and to be impossible without sensation . . ." (*De anima*, III, 428b11–12).

75   *De anima*, 429b429b3–4. Cf. 427b15. *De Generatione animalium,*.

76   Will, latin *voluntas*, does not have a precise corresponding term in Greek. However, in *SCG*, II, 60 [5], Aquinas, interpreting Aristotle's *De anima*, III, 432b5–8, uses *voluntas* for the Greek *boulesis*. The passage in Aristotle reads: "For there is will in the calculative, and desire and passion in the irrational part; and if the soul is divided into three, appetite will be found in each."

77   "But what shall I now say that I am, when I am supposing that there is some supremely powerful . . . deceiver. . . . Since now I do not have a body. . . . Sense-perception? This surely does not occur without a body . . ." (AT VII, 26–27; CSM II, 18).

the difference between imagination and pure understanding in the following way:

> when I imagine a triangle, for example, I do not merely understand that it is a figure bounded by three lines, but at the same time I also see the three lines with my mind's eye as if they were present before me; and this is what I call imagining. But if I want to think of a chiliagon, although I understand that it is a figure consisting of a thousand sides just as well as I understand the triangle to be a three-sided figure, I do not in the same way imagine the thousand sides or see them as if they were present before me.[78]

Let me use another example. Draw on a board 2 dots, 3 dots, 4 dots, 5 dots, 6 dots, 7 dots and so on, in the following way:

```
          *  *
        *  *  *
      *  *  *  *
    *  *  *  *  *
  *  *  *  *  *  *
*  *  *  *  *  *  *
* * * * * * * *
```

We do not have any problems with grasping by means of the "body's eye" the number of 2, 3, 4, 5, or even, 6 dots. However, as the number of dots increases (say, over 6), we can no longer see "clearly and distinctly" the number of dots. We need to count them to know how many of them there are. However, when we are thinking of the number 7 or 8 or any greater number, like a thousand, we know the nature of this number with the same clarity as when we are thinking of the number 2 or 3. In other words, with the increase in complexity of the structure of a visualized, corporeal object, the imagination falls behind understanding in recognizing what the object is. As a matter of fact, imagination proves itself useless very quickly. Therefore, Descartes asks rhetorically, one can wonder whether the imagination is in fact a "constituent" for the essence of the mind.[79] Descartes's answer is in the negative.

78 AT VII 72; CSM II, 50.
79 AT VII 73; CSM II 51.

Therefore, sensory perceptions demonstrate the impossibility of proving the existence of material things. Sensations and imaginations are part of the mind *insofar* as I have a body, but my knowledge of my having it, again, is contingent upon my experience of having a body. However, the *ego*, as a thing that thinks, denies, and wills, is independent of the body. Like Plato (in the *Meno*), Descartes infers that mathematical knowledge is independent of the knowledge of the external world.

What we are dealing with at the beginning of the Sixth Meditation is criticism of the Aristotelian-Thomistic account of mathematics. In Aristotle and Aquinas, the function of the mind is to abstract mathematical ideas from material objects. The way it works is the following: "forms" are "abstracted from the senses," "in so far as the realities it knows are capable of being separated from their matter, so it is also with the powers of mind,"[80] therefore, the mind, although independent of material reality in the sense of not being a sense organ, is nothing[81] before it makes contact with the corporeal world by means of the senses. In Descartes, mathematics, and thus the speculative mind, if one is allowed to

80 *The Exposition of Boethius's* On the Trinity, Art. 2, Response [p. 116]; cf. *On Being and Essence*, Part 3. Cf. *De anima*, III, 429b22–24; cf. 429b10–20. And: "The so-called abstract objects the mind thinks just as, if one had thought of the snub-nosed not as snub-nosed but as hollow, one would have thought of an actuality without the flesh in which it is embodied; it is thus that the mind when it is thinking the objects of Mathematics thinks as separate, elements which do not exist separately. in every case the mind which is actively thinking is the objects which it thinks. *Whether it is possible for it while not existing separate from spatial conditions to think anything that is separate*, or not, we must consider later." 431b13–20. The part of the sentence in italics is a very eloquent declaration of the Aristotelian theory of the dependence of mathematics on sensible perception. Cf. St. Thomas's *Commentary on Aristotle's De anima*, Lecture VIII (Intellectual Abstraction), Translated by Kenelm Foster and Silvester Humphries (Notre Dame, Ind.: Dumb Ox Books, 1994), pp. 211–18.

81 *De anima*, III, 429b–30–31. And: "For this reason it [the intellective soul] cannot reasonably be regarded as blended with the body. . . . It was a good idea to call the soul 'the place of forms,' though (1) this description holds only of the intellective soul, and (2) even this is the forms only potentially, not actually" (*De anima*, III, 429a23–29). Cf. the sentence from Aristotle's *De anima*, III, 431b13–20.

apply an Aristotelian concept with reference to Descartes, is epistemologically prior to the material world. Hence Descartes's difficulty in proving (as opposed to demonstrating[82]) the existence of the material world. All we can say from the Cartesian perspective – the perspective of the severed epistemological link between the potential mind and matter without which the mind cannot become actual – is that "material things exist *in so far* they are the subject matter of pure mathematics."[83] For Aristotle and Aquinas, to paraphrase Descartes, the mind exists insofar as the material world exists.

IV

As I remarked before, the unity of man as a rational animal in Aristotle and Aquinas is guaranteed by the oneness of the human form/soul, which is vegetative, sensitive, and rational at the same time. This tripartite character of the Aristotelian soul does not mean that the soul is composed of three distinct parts which are joined together. The soul, though it performs three functions, is one. Each form of life, be it plants, animals, or men, have appropriate souls, which make them plants, animals, or men, respectively. The rejection of any of the functions, as Descartes does in the Second Meditation by dismissing the vegetative and sensitive parts, would be impossible in the Aristotelian-Thomistic account without destroying that of which it is the form, i.e., man.

Why does it work for Descartes? Clearly, the Cartesian mind is not responsible for the organization of matter, nor is it the body's "act of being" (one of the functions of the Aristotelian-Thomistic form). In Aristotle, thinking is dependent on the bodily organs (which provide the mind with a *phantasm*); in Descartes it is not.

Nowhere is the difference between Aristotle and Descartes more visible than in the Sixth Meditation, where both points – the irreducibility of the Aristotelian soul to Cartesian consciousness and the absence of the rational soul from the body of the Cartesian man – can best be seen.

82 As Descartes himself admits in Meditation V, external objects are similar to the ideas we have of them.
83 AT VII, 71; CSM, II, 50.n

> I might consider the body of *man* as a kind of machine
> equipped with and made up of bones, nerves, muscles,
> veins, blood and skin in such a way that, *even if there*
> *were no mind in it*, it would still perform all the same
> movements as it now does in those cases where movement
> is not under the control of the will or, consequently, of the
> mind. [84]

In both the *De anima*, III, and *De motu animalium* Aristotle is
concerned with the question of movement of (human and non-
human) animals. The movement of animals, Aristotle writes in the
De motu animalium,

> is like that of automatic puppets, which are set moving
> when a small motion occurs: the cables are released and the
> pegs strike against one another. . . . For they have function-
> ing parts that are of the same kind: the sinews and bones.
> The latter are like the pegs and the iron in our example, the
> sinews like the cables. When these are released and slack-
> ened, the creature moves. Now in the puppets . . . no alter-
> ation takes place. . . . But in the animal the same part has
> the capacity to become both larger and smaller and to
> change its shape, as the parts expand because of heat and
> contract again because of cold, and alter.

> Alteration is caused by *phantasias* and sense perceptions
> and ideas. For sense-perceptions are at once a kind of alter-
> ation and *phantasiai* and thinking have the power of the
> actual things. For it turns out that form conceived of [warm
> or cold or] pleasant or fearful is like the actual thing itself.
> That is why we shudder and are frightened just thinking of
> something. . . . Now the origin of motion is, as we have said,
> the object of pursuit or avoidance in the sphere of action.
> Of necessity the thought and *phantasia* of these are accom-
> panied by heating and chilling. For the painful is avoided
> and the pleasant pursued, and the thought and *phantasia*
> of the painful and the pleasant are nearly always accompa-
> nied by chilling and heating. . . . That is why it is pretty
> much at the same time that the creature thinks it should
> move forward and moves, unless something else impedes it.
> For the affections suitably prepare the organic parts, desire
> the affections, and *phantasia* the desire; and *phantasia*

84   AT, VII, 84; CSM, II, 58.

comes about either through thought or through sense-perception . . .[85]

Given the confines of this chapter, it is impossible to give a full account of Aristotle's extremely complicated theory here.[86] I would like to make, however, a few points. The citation from Aristotle may sound reminiscent of Descartes's description of man's body from the Sixth Meditation, and one can safely presume, I think,[87] that it was this passage from the *De motu animalium* Descartes thought of while writing his description of the body of a man in the Sixth Meditation. Similar as those two passages might appear at first glance, there are, however, a few points which make the two accounts incompatible. First, unlike Descartes, Aristotle does not think blood is an animating principle of the animal's movement. Although the essential parts of Aristotle's animal, including the human animal, like that of the Cartesian man, are mechanical pieces, the cause of its movement is *phantasia* or thought. Of course, to make thinking the principle of animal movement, thought must be understood differently than it is understood by Descartes. "Now we see that the movers of the animal, Aristotle writes, are reasoning and *phantasia* and choice and wish and appetite. And all of these can be reduced to thought and desire. For both *phantasia* and sense-perception hold the same place as thought, since all are concerned with making distinctions – though they differ from each other in ways we have discussed elsewhere."[88] The "elsewhere" takes us back to an earlier work, *De anima*. Before I move on to this text, let me make the following remark. Aristotle's major concern, both in the *De anima* and in *De motu animalium*, but also in *De somnio*, is the following: in what sense is the soul responsible for movement? In commenting on *De*

85 701b34–702a19. Martha Craven Nussbaum, *Aristotle's* De Motu Animalium. *Text with Translation, Commentary and Interpretive Essay* (Princeton, N.J.: Princeton University Press, 1978).

86 The reader should consult Martha Craven Nussbaum's excellent discussion in her *Aristotle's* De Motu animalium: *Text with Translation, Commentary and Interpretive Essay* (Princeton, N.J.: Princeton University Press, 1978).

87 Cf. Aristotle 702b13ff and AT VII, 87; CSM II, 60.

88 *De motu animalium*, 700b17–23. See also, 704a18–21.

motu animalium, 2, 259b1–15, Martha Nussbaum suggests that if self-motion (as Hardie and Gaye claim) requires external stimuli, then it is not self-motion properly speaking.[89] Although Nussbaum does not say that directly, she is correct: if the only genuine sort of self-movement is movement that is not caused by the external stimuli (*phantasm*), then no animal in Aristotle should have souls. This, of course, runs counter to everything Aristotle maintains. Having said that, we can pose the following question: if both animals and men have souls (which are responsible for self-movement), what is the difference between man and animal *if* both need a phantasm to initiate movement?

According to Aristotle (in the *De anima*), the animal soul is characterized by (1) the faculty of discrimination[90] (which is the work of thought and sense) and (2) the faculty of originating local movement.[91] What does originate "forward movement" in the animal?[92] Not the nutritive faculty – Aristotle answers, because the nutritive faculty belongs both to plants and animals.[93] Having ruled out the nutritive faculty as a source of movement, Aristotle remarks that forward movement is for the sake of an *end* and "is accompanied either by [1] imagination or by [2] appetite."[94] However, "neither can the calculative faculty or that which is called 'mind' (*logistikon kai to kaloumenos nous*) be the cause of such movement; for the mind as speculative never thinks what is practicable; it never says anything about an object to be avoided or pursued, while this movement is always in something which is avoiding or pursuing an object."[95] Again, having ruled out the speculative mind as the source of movement, Aristotle moves on to appetite. But again, he remarks, "appetite too is incompetent to account *fully* for movement; for those who successfully resist temptation have appetite and desire and yet follow the mind [nous] and refuse to enact that for which they have appetite."[96] Note,

89 *Ibid.*, pp. 119ff.
90 *De anima*, III, 42913–14.
91 *De anima*, III, 432a15–19.
92 *De anima*, III, 432b14.
93 *De anima*, 433a9–13 and 428b11–12.
94 *De anima*, 432b15–16.
95 *De anima*, III, 432b27–29.
96 *De anima*, 433a6–9.

Aristotle does not claim that appetite is not a source of movement; it is, but only in animals, whereas in man, insofar as man is capable of acting contrary to appetite, there must be another, additional, source of movement. "These two at all events appear to be source of movement: appetite and mind."97 What kind of mind is this? Aristotle remarks that one may "venture to regard imagination as a kind of thinking," which, in turn, is "impossible without sensation,"98 and consequently without a body. In conclusion, Aristotle states: ""inasmuch as an animal is capable of appetite it is capable of self-movement; it is not capable of appetite without possessing imagination; and all imagination is either (1) calculative or (2) sensitive. In the latter all animals, and not only man, partake."99 In short, what differentiates man from animals is the "practical mind" which "calculates" a means to an end.100

If one could solicit Aristotle's or Aquinas's reaction to the description of the human body in the Sixth Meditation, they would most likely say this: First, is this a description of a *human* body? After all, if one replaces the word *"man's* body" in the above passage with the name of any animal, say an ape, what Descartes claims to be a description of a human body is a description of the body of *any* animal. Second, insofar as it is a human body, man must have a calculative imagination.101

If the human body in the above quoted passage can move without speculative imagination, what Descartes claims to be a man is not a man, even though the shape of his body is human, but an animal. What we witness in the Sixth Meditation is an act of "lobotomy": Descartes deprived (his) man of the "calculative imagination" which is proper only to humans.102

Descartes's second major concern in the Sixth Meditation is the so-called "the teaching of Nature,"103 which I will call, respectively Part I and Part II. According to Part I,

97 *De anima*, 433a10–11.
98 *De anima*, 428b11–12.
99 *De anima*, 433b28–31.
100 *De anima*, 433b30.
101 *De anima*, 433b27–31; 434a5–6.
102 *De anima*, 433b30.
103 For a general account of the "Teaching of Nature," see Richard

> [1] There is nothing that my own nature teaches me more
> vividly than that I have a body, and that when I am hungry
> or thirsty the body needs food and drink, and so on. . . . My
> nature . . . does indeed teach me to avoid what induces a
> feeling of pain and to seek out what induces feelings of
> pleasure, and so on.

The Teaching of Nature comes down to a simple precept: avoiding
pain and seeking pleasure. The Cartesian Teaching of Nature finds
a counterpart in the *De anima* and the *De motu animalium*, where
Aristotle also talks about what "object [should] be avoided or pursued."[104] Again, like Descartes, Aristotle is concerned with what
causes the movement of bodies,[105] of which, he says, there are two
sources: "appetite," which induces animals to move, and the "calculative" mind, which induces men to move. Now, insofar as the
body of Cartesian man can move without a mind, the Teaching of
Nature is an account of the movement which in Aristotle results
from "appetite," i.e., the movement of animals.

In Part II of the Teaching of Nature Descartes attempts to re-
establish the mind's connection with the body:

> [2] Nature also teaches me, by these sensations of pain,
> hunger, thirst and so on, that I am not merely present in my
> body as a sailor is present in a ship, but that I am very
> closely joined and, as it were, intermingled with it, so that
> I and the body form a unit.

Let me stress this point: this is the only argument in the entire
Cartesian corpus for the substantial union of the Cartesian soul
and body.

> – Let me juxtapose this passage to a short fragment from
> Plato's *Phaedo* (83c-8):
> – That the soul of every man, when it feels violent pleasure
> or pain in connection with some object, inevitably believes
> at the same time that what causes such feelings must be
> very clear and very true, which it is not. Such objects are
> mostly visible, are they not?

Kennington, "The Teaching of Nature in Descartes's Soul Doctrine," *The
Review of Metaphysics*, 1972, Vol. XXVI, No. 1, pp. 86–117.

104 *De anima*, 433a14, and throughout the *De motu animalium*.
105 "[forward] movement is always in something which is avoiding or pursuing an object" (432b27–29).

– Certainly.

– And doesn't such an experience tie the soul to the body most completely?

– How so?

– Because every pleasure and every pain provides, as it were, another nail to rivet the soul to the body and to weld them together. It makes the soul corporeal, so that it believes that truth is what the body says it is. As it shares the beliefs and delights of the body, I think it inevitably comes to share its ways and manner of life and is unable ever to reach Hades in a pure state; it is always full of body when it departs, so that it soon falls back into another body and grows with it as if it had been sewn into it. Because of this, it can have no part in the company of the divine, the pure and uniform.

The above argument for the connection between the body and the soul is typical of what we find in other Platonic dialogues. We do not know exactly how the soul is connected to the body: it is, to follow Plato's metaphorical language, nailed or welded to the body. But we know that it is connected because we experience pleasure and pain. How does this explanation differ from that of Descartes? I am not sure it does, and if it does not, Descartes is subject to the same criticism that Aquinas applied to Plato's argument.[106]

Although Aquinas who invented the sailor metaphor against Platonic epistemology and anthropology never had the chance to read the *Phaedo*,[107] where pleasure and pain are the signs of the

106 With one exception, however. As far as the existence of Ideas is concerned, Descartes would not agree with Plato. His conception of the dependence of the eternal truths on God makes Descartes an unlikely cognitive Platonist. However, since Descartes had not laid out the doctrine of the eternal truths in the *Meditations*, readers might have had reason to suspect him of at least anthropological Platonism. Literature on this topic is hardly existent. However, readers interested in epistemological Platonism in Descartes should consult Tad Schmaltz, "Platonism and Descartes's View of Immutable Essences," in *Archiv Fur Geschichte Der Philosophie*. 73, 1991 (2), pp. 154ff. Schmaltz does not discuss in detail Descartes's relationship to Plato. However, it is a good defense of the mistaken Platonist reading of Descartes suggested by Kenny, Gueroult, and Gewirth.

107 The transmission of the Platonic tradition from Antiquity to the Middle Ages is discussed by Raymond Klibansky in his *The Continuity of the*

union, one might say that in inventing his metaphor he precluded any possibility of conceiving pleasure and pain as the nail joining the soul and body in a substantial union. Descartes may have claimed that this union is substantial; however, there is nothing in his explanation that, first, says how this union is different from the Platonic one, and, second, would help us to understand how the union can be substantial if the mind does not need the body to transfer the phantasm to activate the (active) intellect.

Let me make one final point. How do I know that I have a body, in Aristotle? The question is somewhat spurious considering the "givenness" of the external world in Aristotle. At the end of the *De anima* (433a-435b26), Aristotle is concerned with the question of what serves the preservation of body. However, in contradistinction to Descartes, whose primary goal is to account for the union between the body and the soul, Aristotle is concerned with the question of the purpose of having the five senses. Each sense, he says, apprehends one aspect of a sensible thing. Were we to apprehend everything by means of a special organ, instead of separate senses, each of which accounts for one aspect of a sensible, we would, for example, always think of yellow as bitter, as in the case of bile which happens to be yellow. Thus everything would merge into an indistinguishable identity.[108] Aristotle's next point is the following. While everything must have nutritive soul, sensation is proper only to animals who are capable of forward movement (as opposed to stationary living things[109] which receive nutriment from which they have arisen). The sense of touch is primary (but also taste, which is a form of touch), which is indispensable for

Platonic Tradition during the Middle Ages (London: The Warburg Institute, 1939). New expanded edition, which includes an additional part on *Plato's* Parmenides *in the Middle Ages and the Renaissance*, was published by Kraus International Publications (Millwood, 1981). A much more detailed treatment of the Platonic tradition in the Middle Ages can be found in Stefan Swiezawski's "*Homo platonicus* w wiekach srednich" (*Homo Platoniucs* in the Middle Ages), *Roczniki Filozoficzne* (Lublin [Poland], 1949–50), pp. 250–97. Although the main body of this article is in Polish, and therefore inaccessible for most scholars, the article may prove very useful since all citations from Medieval writers are in Latin.

108 *De anima*, 425b7–9.

109 *De anima*, 434b2ff.

survival.[110] The sense of hearing, seeing and smell, are innutritious. Yet, they are indispensable if an animal is to survive, since it must perceive objects from a distance. Hence Aristotle concludes: "All the other senses are necessary to animals . . . not for their being, but for their well-being."[111]

110 *De anima*, 433b11ff.
111 *De anima*, 435b19–20.

Cartesian Circle of Friends

Thomas Aquinas

Le Cardinal de Berulle

Cardinal Berulle

Admodum Reuerendus Pater Guillelmus Gibieuf Congregationis Oratorij Domini Iesu Præsbiter et in
eâ administranda Emi. Cardinalis Berulli quod vixit Prouicarius Necnon in Regendo Virginum
Carmelitanum per Galliam Vniuersam Ordinis, ipsius Meritissimus successor Doctor Sorbonicus
inter splendidissima sæculi sui lumina iure censendus, vir acerrimi judicij, ingenij celerrimi,
suspiciendæ eruditionis, et quod cunctis his dotibus facile præferas, eximiæ et synceræ
in Deum pietatis. Obiit 6 Iunij anno domini 1650.   Ph. Champagne pin. L. Boulanger sc.

Guillaume Gibieuf

Adrien Baillet

Guy de Balzac

Marin Mersenne

Antoine Arnauld

Queen Christina of Sweden

Queen Elizabeth of Bohemia

Blaise Pascal

Charles de Condren

Général de la Congregat.on de l'Oratoire né au
village de Vaubuin pres Soissons l'an 1588.
mort a Paris   l'an 1641.

E. Desrochers fecit et exc. rue du Fou pres la rue S. Jacques   Paris

Fondateur du Collége de Juilly
érigé en Académie royale
par Lettres patentes de Louis XIII
du mois d'Avril 1638.

Charles de Condren of the Oratory

Jean Morin, Pere de
l'oratoire né à Blois et decedé
à Paris le 28. Fevrier 1659. agé
de 68. ans

Gravé par B.Desrochers rue du Foin prés. la rue St. Jacques a Paris.

Le Ciel ayant tiré ce vaste et grand genie
De l'abisme ou l'erreur l'avoit precipité.
Ce Saint Prestre employa Sa science infinie
En faveur de la Verité.

Jean Morin of the Oratory

How to Read Descartes's Third Meditation: On Descartes's Alleged Debt to Duns Scotus[1]

The most immediate consequence of the Cartesian Doubt in the First Meditation is that it renders St. Thomas Aquinas's cosmological proof for the existence of God useless: if our sensory apparatus is not reliable, one cannot, as did St. Thomas Aquinas, build a proof that rests on the premise that things *in* the world move and proceed to the demonstration of the cause of their movement. In other words, according to Descartes, for all we know, the world may not exist, and one cannot argue for the existence of the First Cause from a supposition which in itself is dubious.

Although Descartes does not explicitly make St. Thomas's proof the target of his enterprise, his remarks to Caterus, his comments in his letters,[2] but above all, the implications of his method show that St. Thomas's proof was an implicit target of Descartes's own proof. In his *First Set of Replies* to Caterus, Descartes was compelled to explain his position vis-à-vis that of Aquinas.[3] I did

---

1   An earlier version of this chapter was presented as a lecture at the University of King's College, Halifax, Canada, in November 2003.
2   See Descartes's letter to Voetius of May 1643 (AT VIIIB, 175; CSMK III, 170): "St. Thomas's arguments against the atheists have, on closer examination, been found to be invalid. . . . I wrote against atheists and put forward my arguments as first rate."
3   For an analysis of Caterus/Descartes exchange with respect to medieval tradition, and St. Thomas in particular, see Emanuela Scribano,

not base my argument on the observation of the order of efficient causes "perceived by the senses," Descartes says because, first, I regard the existence of God to be "much more evident than the existence of anything that can be perceived by the senses"; second, Aquinas's proof, Descartes continues, "could not lead me anywhere except to a recognition of the imperfection of my intellect, since an infinite chain of such successive causes from eternity without any first cause is beyond my grasp."[4] And that is how he explains his position: "my inability to grasp it certainly does not entail that there must be a first cause, any more than my inability to grasp the infinite number of divisions in a finite quantity entails that there is an ultimate division beyond which any further division is impossible."[5]

The first part of Descartes's argument is the unfolding of the consequences of Doubt in the First Meditation (sensory perceptions are unreliable; therefore, the proof for God's existence cannot be based on "efficient causality"). The second part of the argument – touching on the infinite divisibility beyond which something becomes indivisible – is of a logical, rather than procedural, nature.

Because the cosmological proof is of no avail to Descartes, the only way left to demonstrate the existence of God is from the contents of the (disembodied) self. In addressing the proof for the existence of God in the Third Meditation, Descartes raises the following question: "From whom . . . would I derive my existence? From myself presumably, or from my parents . . ." The answer to both questions is in the negative: "[I]f I derived my existence from myself . . . I should have given myself all the perfections of which I have any idea, and thus I should myself be God . . ." "[A]s regards my parents, even if everything I have ever believed about them is true, it is certainly not they who, [first], preserve me; and, [second], in so far as I am a thinking thing, they did not even make me; they merely placed certain dispositions in the matter which I have always regarded as containing me, or rather my mind, for that is all

L'existence de Dieu: Histoire de la preuve ontologique de Descartes à Kant (Paris: Seuil, 2002), pp. 65–82.
4   AT VII 106; CSM II, 77.
5   AT VII 106; CSM II, 77.

I now take myself to be."[6] In his *Reply* to Caterus, Descartes explains: "I preferred to use my own existence as the basis of my argument [for the existence of God], since it does not depend on any chain of causes. . . . And the question I asked concerning myself was not what was the cause that originally produced me, but what is the cause that preserves me . . . in inquiring about what caused me, I was asking about myself, not in so far as I consist of mind and body, but only and precisely in so far as I am a thinking thing."[7]

Descartes dismisses biological parenthood for two reasons. First, Descartes is not concerned here with (his) existence understood as the existence of the composite of mind and body: the meaning of the word existence in the question – what is the source of my *existence?* – refers to the mind, reason, or intellect – must shift from existence understood in biological terms to a non-biological source. However, from the fact that my parents are not my parents, metaphysically speaking, it does not follow that God is. Already in the First Meditation, after considering the possibility that the sky, the Earth, and, consequently, my body may not exist, Descartes considers the possibility of his coming into being as a result of chance, fate, or a series of causes. In other words, the argument from the Second Meditation that he is a *res cogitans* does not by itself yield the proof for the existence of God. In other words, while the Universal Doubt establishes the existence of the *res cogitans*, the proof for the existence of God requires a separate demonstration.

Descartes does not go into details about what exactly the notion of dependence means. In the most philosophically widespread sense, the notion of dependence means that a contingent being needs a non-contingent source. The Medievals' argument is this: I am not a necessary being, that is, a being whose essence *is* his existence. Only in the case of such a being cannot the essence be separated from existence. I, on the other hand, exist only because God "lent" me an act of being, as Aquinas would have it[8];

6   AT VII, 52–52, CSM II, 35.
7   AT VII, 107; CSM II, 77.
8   *Commentary on the Sentences* I, Art. 1, Ad. 2: "the creature exists only to the degree that it descends from the primary being, and it is called

if He were to remove the act of existence from me, I would cease to be. In Aquinas an act of being, which is the soul, is different from the essence of man. "The human soul is a form and an act," Aquinas writes in *Summa Contra Gentiles*, II, 81, "which was joined to [the body] according to one act of being, with body" (*anima humana est forma et actus . . . anima unitur corpori secundum esse unum*). Accordingly, the soul, or *anima*, is the form of a body, the act of existence of a body, and therefore cannot be separated from it without destroying man, i.e., the composite.

Can the act of existence, as Aquinas understood it, be separated from the Cartesian man? In Descartes, the *res cogitans* is not the essence of man, that is, the composite of mind and body; on the contrary, *res cogitans* is the essence of me insofar as I do not have this body which is the source of sense perceptions and imagination. In the Sixth Meditation Descartes emphatically states: "I consider that this power of imagining which is in me, differing as it does from the power of understanding, *is not a necessary constituent of my own essence, that is, the essence of my mind*."[9] If we link this passage with the definition of the *res cogitans* in the Second Meditation things become clearer: unlike imagination and sensory perceptions, which require a body, doubting, understanding, affirming, denial, and willing and its opposite, do not. The Cartesian mind, insofar as it can be separated from the body, is not an act of existence of the body, as it is in Aquinas. As a matter of fact, it does not need to be because, in contradistinction to

being only because it imitates the first being." Edited and translated by Ralph McInerny (London: Penguin, 1998), p. 58. Cf. Duns Scotus, *De primo principio*, 3.26, 3.22, 3.19.

9   AT VII, 73; CSM, II, 51 (emphasis mine). See also, VII, 28; CSM II, 19: "I thus realize that none of the things that the imagination enables me to grasp is at all relevant to this knowledge of myself which I possess, and that the mind must therefore be most carefully diverted from such things *if it is to perceive its own nature* as distinctly as possible" (emphasis mine).

"But what then am I? A thing that thinks. What is that? A thing that (1) doubts, (2) understands, (3) affirms, (4) denies, is (5) willing, is unwilling, and also (6) imagines and has (7) sensory perceptions." Since I may not have this body which I call mine, (6) and (7) are only conditional, as it were, components of what I am.

Aquinas, the Cartesian mind is not (necessarily)[10] the body's *animating* principle: it neither animates it, nor is it the principle of the body's organization; what animates the body of the Cartesian man is blood.[11] If the *anima* is not necessary to animate the body, Cartesian *res cogitans* is not man's act of existence; Cartesian mind is a replica of God – it is an individual act of existence which reflects God's image in itself. Cartesian *ego* is the *imago Dei*. This reading is reflected in the text of the *Meditations*, where Descartes states that "what caused me is itself a thinking thing"(. . . *illam etiam esse rem cogitantem* . . .).[12] Descartes's proof for the existence of God is an attempt to explain where this reflection (*imago Dei*) or idea of God that is in me came from.

In the language of the Third Meditation, Descartes's argument

10   "I might consider the body of a man as a kind of machine equipped with and made up of bones, nerves, muscles, veins, blood and skin in such a way that, *even if there were no mind in it*, it would still perform all the same movements as it now does in those cases where movement is not under the control of the will or, consequently, of the mind." Med VI, AT VII, 84; CSM II, 58.

11   Let me make a parenthetical remark here. Descartes devoted the Fifth Discourse to blood circulation. At first glance, the theme of the Fifth Discourse is rather surprising. However, it ceases to be so if we recall that the Fourth Discourse is, as Descartes tells Mersenne (Letter to Mersenne, 27 February 1637 [AT I, 350; CSMK I, 186]) a "summary" of his philosophy, that is, the *Meditations*. In the Sixth Meditation we witness the birth of Modern (Cartesian) Man whose body is a piece of mechanism. Insofar as its movements are concerned, they may proceed from the soul, as Descartes admits, but they can be explained in mechanical terms as well. Accordingly, if one can dispense with the Scholastic *anima* as a form of explanation of the movements of man's body in favor of a mechanical account, since this body would display the same behavior "even if there were no mind [or soul] in it," thus blood pumped through the veins of Cartesian Man becomes the source of movement. This is why the Fifth Discourse is devoted to blood circulation. What I would like to propose is to read Descartes's oeuvres in the following order: the First, Second, and Third Discourse, then the six *Meditations* in place of the Fourth Discourse, which is an abbreviation of it, and move on to Discourse 5 and 6. The Fifth Discourse provides us with an alternative explanation as to what can be a source of the body's movement to the traditional *anima*, namely, blood. The Sixth Discourse, not surprisingly, culminates in a rejection of the old speculative philosophy taught in the Schools in favor of the project of practical philosophy and the mastery of nature.

12   Med III, AT VII, 49; CSM II, 34.

for the existence of God amounts to the following point: I cannot be the source of an idea of an infinite being; hence, this being must have imprinted the idea or image of Himself in my mind.

Descartes unfolds his proof for the existence of God by bringing in a battery of Scholastic terms: "objective," "formal," and "eminent" reality, "potential" and "objective" being. Cartesian scholars have been looking for the source or sources of Descartes's vocabulary, particularly his use of the "objective reality," since the publication of Gilson's magisterial works. So far, the majority of research has been centered primarily on Suarez.[13] As Timothy Cronin, who devoted probably what can be considered to be the most thorough analysis of this term in Descartes and Suarez,[14] wrote: "Whatever the historical precedents may have been, the doctrine of the objective reality of ideas cannot possibly lie on a line of doctrine common to Descartes and the Scholastics. There will always remain a discontinuity in doctrine between Descartes and that of any scholastic."[15] In the past few decades, other scholars brought to our

13 To mention the most important ones, the interested reader should consult: Roland Dalbiez, "Les sources scolastiques de la théorie cartésienne de l'être objectif: A Propos du 'Descartes' de M. Gilson," in *Revue d'Histoire de la philosophie* 3, pp. 464–72; Timothy J. Cronin, *Objective Being in Descartes and in Suarez* (Rome: Gregorian University Press, 1966); Calvin Normore, "Meaning and Objective Being: Descartes and His Sources," in *Essays on Descartes'* Meditations, Amélie Oksenberg Rorty ed. (Berkeley: University of California Press, 1986), pp. 223–43; Marco Forlivesi, "La distinction entre concept formèl et concept objectif: Suarez, Pasqualigo, Mastri," in *Les Études Philosophiques*, 1 (2002); Jean-François Courtine, "La doctrine cartésienne de l'idée et ses sources scolastiques," *Les catégories de l'être: Etudes de philosophie ancienne et médiévale* (Paris: PUF, 2003). See also Roger Ariew, *Descartes and the Last Scholastics* (Ithaca, N.Y., and London: Cornell University Press, 1999), pp. 39–57. For an analysis of the proof for the existence of God, see Olivier Boulnois, "Preuve de Dieu et structure de la métaphysique selon Duns Scotus," in *Revue des Sciences Philosophique et Théologiques*, vol. 83, No. 1 (January 1999).

14 Timothy J. Cronin, *Objective Being in Descartes and in Suarez* (Rome: Gregorian University Press, 1966).

15 Timothy Cronin, "Objective Reality of Idea in Human Thought: Descartes and Suarez," in *Wisdom in Depth: Essays in Honor of Henri Renard*, V. Daues, M. Holloway, L. Sweeney eds. (Milwaukee: The Bruce Publishing Company, 1966), pp. 68–69.

attention other texts which Descartes might have been familiar with. However, not much attention has been paid to Duns Scotus, and less so to the philosophers' use of "eminent" and "formal" reality. In two of his works, *De primo principio* and *De esse Dei*, there are a number of passages where we find the notions of *eminent* and *formal* reality, but also, on a number of occasions Scotus's considerations and examples bear some resemblance to Descartes's own considerations in the Third Meditation.

In a familiar passage from *De esse Dei*, which forms part of his *Ordinatio*,[16] Scotus writes: "[A] son depends upon his father for existence but is not dependent upon him in exercising his own causality, since he can act just as well whether his father be living or dead."[17] Let me illustrate Scotus's point by the following example. Imagine a series of balls, A, B, C, D, etc. If ball A hits ball B, ball A will impart its force on ball B, making it move; B in turn will impart its force on C, making it move in turn, and so on. For ball B to move, A has to impart its movement on B, but once A has done this, B rolls on its own even when ball A stops moving. Take ball C, for example. One of the implications here is this: the movement of C is an effect of B, but looked at from the point of view of D, C is the cause of the movement of D. Thus each element of the series can be considered to be a cause and an effect. There is only one element in this series which is only a cause, namely, the first one.

The sentence from Scotus that I quoted above was taken from

16   There are two works by Scotus that Descartes might have used: *Ordinatio* (of which *De esse Dei* is a part) and *De primo principio*. According to traditional view, the latter work is Scotus's early work. There are many overlapping passages in both works, which can be cross-referenced. Therefore, although the majority of quotations from Scotus in the main body of this chapter I cite from his *Ordinatio*, the ones which find their counterparts in *De primo principio* will be referred to in the footnotes.

17   Duns Scotus, *De esse Dei*, in *Philosophical Writings*, bilingual edition (Cambridge, Mass.: Hackett, 1987), pp. 40–41. For the corresponding passage, see *De primo principio*, 3.14. For the use of the same example in Ockham ("quia filius generat patre mortuo sicut vivo"), see Ockham, *Questiones in lib. I Physicorum*, Q. cxxxv, Latin text and English translation by P. Boehner (Cambridge, Mass.: Hackett, 1990), p. 120; Suarez, *Disputatio* 29 [25], in *The Metaphysical Demonstration of the Existence of God*, tr. by John P. Doyle (South Bend, Ind.: St. Augustine's Press, 2004), p. 68.

a passage in which Scotus draws a contrast between two kinds of causality: *accidental* and *essential*. Scotus explains the difference between the two in the following way:

> In essentially ordered causes, the second depends upon the first precisely in its act of causation.[18] In accidentally ordered causes this is not the case, although the second may depend upon the first for its existence or in some other way. Thus a son depends upon his father for existence but is not dependent upon him in exercising his own causality, since he can act just as well whether his father be living or dead.[19] The second difference is that in essentially ordered causes the causality is of another nature and order, *inasmuch as the higher cause is more perfect*. Such is not the case, however, with accidentally ordered causes.[20]

And Scotus adds:

> [By] reason of the second difference, the higher cause is more perfect in its causality, therefore what is infinitely higher is infinitely more perfect and hence of infinite perfection. Now nothing infinitely perfect can cause something only in virtue of another, because everything of this kind is imperfect in its causality since it depends on another in order to cause its effect.[21]

If in essentially ordered causes the higher cause is more perfect, in accidentally ordered causes, this is not necessarily the case. Thus, for example, John (the father) can be a genius, while Mark (the son) can be an idiot. Or vice versa: Mark can be a genius whereas John can be an idiot; and if Mark happens to have his

18 Cf. Aristotle, *Physics*, VIII, 5, and St. Thomas, *Summa Theologica*, I, 46. 2 and 7.

19 Cf. *De primo principio*, 3.13. In 2.44, Scotus remarks, after Artistotle (in *Metaphysics*, IX), that "what is generated depends upon what went on before." Accordingly, Descartes's claim to the effect that he did not derive his existence from his parents, means that within the framework of his discussion, he can bypass the Aristotelian idea of generation. But also, when he states that insofar as I did not derive my existence from my parents, who are the authors of my bodily constitution, Descartes implies that the substantial union between the body and the mind is outside of his consideration.

20 *Ibid.*, pp. 40–42. Cf. *De primo principio*: 3.10, 3.11, 3.12, 3.13, 3.14.

21 *De esse Dei*, *ibid.*, p. 42.

own son, he can be either an idiot or a genius. In accidentally ordered causes, there is no order of perfection, whereas in the essentially ordered causes perfections proceed from the first to the next one.[22] One can call the essentially ordered causes a "diminishing order of perfection," since it is always the case that A possesses more perfection than B, and B possesses more perfection than C, and so on. However, since the source of perfections is always the First Cause, there are in fact only two elements in the essentially ordered causes: the First Cause on the one hand, and the rest (no matter how many elements there are) on the other. Therefore, the backward procession from, say, me, through my parents, and their parents to their parents, and so on, back to the Biblical Adam and Eve, is not going to bring me any closer to the First Cause, that is, God, who created Adam and Eve. My proximity to the First Cause is the same as Adam's. In other words, while in *accidentally* ordered series, D is caused by C, C is caused by B, B is caused by A, in *essentially* ordered series, C is not essentially caused by B, nor is D essentially caused by C. The perfections of B and C and D depend on *eminent* possession of those perfections by the First Cause. In short, the distance between A, the First Cause, and B, the first element of the series, on the one hand, and, on the other hand, the First Cause and D, the last element of the series, is the same, whereas in the accidental series the distance between the First Cause and any given element of the series is measured in terms of the number of intermediate links between them.

Scotus felt it necessary to introduce the distinction between essential and accidental causality because, as he explains in *De primo principio*, 3.14, accidental causality is unable to explain the source of forms. "For no change of form is perpetuated save in virtue of something permanent which is not part of that succession . . ."[23] There is no straightforward transition from what Scotus says here to Descartes, but the reason for Descartes's dismissal of biological parenthood is similar. What the reference to the biological parents cannot explain is their being my parents insofar as I am *res cogitans*. In other words, accidental causality

22 *De primo principio*, III, 3.11.
23 *De primo principio*, 2.32; *De esse Dei, ibid.*, p. 42.

refers to the order of bodies, whereas essential causality obtains in the realm of *res cogitans*.

Descartes's greatest accomplishment, for better or worse, was to reverse the Aristotelian-Scholastic order. For all we know, the world may not exist. Hence one cannot infer, as does Aquinas, the existence of God from the movement of physical objects. If I know that God exists, it is because I am not the author of the idea of the Supreme Being since "I am plainly unable either to take away anything from it or to add anything to it."[24] However, the question arises, where did this idea come from? To understand properly Descartes's position, it is useful to contrast it with its opposite presented by Aquinas. In his *Summa Contra Gentiles*, I, 43 [10], Aquinas writes:

> Our intellect, furthermore, extends to the infinite in understanding; and a sign of this is that, given any finite quantity, our intellect can think of a greater one. But this ordination of the intellect would be in vain unless an infinite intelligible reality existed. There must, therefore, be some infinite intelligible reality, which must be the greatest of beings. This we call God. God is, therefore, infinite.

Aquinas's claim has no application to Descartes's reasoning. Descartes could not say "given any finite quantity" because the Universal Doubt put the existence of finite objects in question. If the Cartesian mind can conceive the idea of infinity, it is only because it is already there; it is not a multiplication of the finite[25] that yields the Infinite which the intellect grasps by leaving the sensible behind. The Cartesian idea of infinity is something positive which I know[26] since I find it in myself. Be that as it may, the question is: how does the existence of God follow from having the idea of Him? According to Caterus, it does not.

In his comment, Caterus makes the following point: "what sort of cause does an idea need? Indeed what *is* an idea?" In response, he writes:

24 AT VII, 51; cf. St. Thomas, *SCG* I, 43 [10]; Cf. *The First Set of Replies*, AT VII, 103–7; CSM II, 75–77.
25 AT VII, 47: CSM II, 32: "it will never actually be infinite, since it will never reach the point where it is not capable of a further increase."
26 On the difference between "knowing" and "grasping" something, see Descartes's Letter to Mersenne, 27 May 1630 (AT I, 152; CSMK III, 25).

> It is the thing that is thought of, in so far as it has *objective*
> being in the intellect (*objective est in intellectu*). But what
> is "*objective* being in the intellect?" According to what I
> was taught, this is simply the determination of an act of the
> intellect by means of an object. And this is merely an extra-
> neous label which adds nothing to the thing itself. Just as
> "being seen" is nothing other than an act of vision attribut-
> able to myself, so "being thought of," or having an objective
> being in the intellect, is simply a thought of the mind which
> stops and terminates in the mind. . . . So, why should I look
> for a cause of something which is not actual . . . for *objec-*
> *tive* reality is a pure label, not anything actual.[27]

"Objective reality," according to Caterus, is an "act" of the intellect, not a "being" in the intellect; as an act, *objective* reality of an
idea does not require a *cause*, since it is the intellect's activity.[28]

If Caterus's presentation is an expression of a genuine
Scholastic position,[29] the disagreement between Descartes and him
stems from the fact that Descartes modified the traditional meaning of "objective being" to fit his proof. In his response to Caterus,
Descartes concedes that insofar as we have in mind objects outside
the intellect, "objective reality" is "an extraneous label."[30]
However, in the very next sentence, he says that "'objective being'
simply means being in the way in which objects are *normally*
there."[31] Now, for example, for an idea of an object, e.g., the sun,
to be "normally" in the intellect it should signify "the object's being
in the intellect: or, the idea of the sun is the sun itself existing in
the intellect – not of course *formally*, as it does in the heavens . . .
it is not therefore simply nothing." In the very next sentence
Descartes insists on the fact that an idea has an "objective reality"

27 AT VII, 92, CSM II, 66–67.
28 In the Third Meditation Descartes writes: "the nature of an idea is such
     that of itself it requires no formal reality . . ." AT VII, 41; CSM II, 28.
29 In his "La réalité objective dans les *Premières objections* aux *Méditations*
     Métaphysiques: Ockham contre Descartes" (*Revue de Métaphysique et*
     de Morale, No. 1 [2000]), Laurence Renault points to Ockham as a possi-
     ble source of Caterus's understanding of "objective reality."
30 "Notice here that he is referring to the thing itself as if it were located out-
     side the intellect, and in this sense 'objective being in the intellect' is cer-
     tainly an extraneous label"; AT VII, 102; CSM II, 74.
31 AT VII, 102; CSM II, 74; emphasis mine.

if it represents something that exists *formally*, as does the sun in the skies. In other words, if an object exists outside the intellect, it is formally there, but the idea of this object has also an "objective reality." In other words, something exists formally if it exists outside the intellect (like the sun or a stone), but an idea of something (the Sun or stone) possesses "objective reality" the same way that any other idea that I am able to conceive does.

The bone of contention between Descartes and Caterus comes down to the following point: if, as Caterus claims, an idea is *conceived* by an intellect, it is not *caused* (and thus it is not actual/*non actu est*), and therefore it does not refer us to a thing outside the intellect; hence "objective reality" is a mere name. For Descartes, on the other hand, all ideas are caused since the mind needs a cause to "conceive" an idea.[32] In other words, what Descartes's position comes down to is blurring the distinction between "being conceived" and "being caused."

Not surprisingly, Descartes's proof did not convince Caterus, who says, "a supremely perfect being carries the implication of existence in virtue of its very title, [however] it still does not follow that the existence in question is anything actual in the real world; all that follows is that the concept of existence is inseparably linked to the concept of a supreme being. So you cannot infer that the existence of God is anything *actual* unless you suppose that the supreme being actually exists."[33]

(Let me make a parenthetical remark here. As Caterus points out to Descartes, St. Thomas, when he considers the proposition "God exists is self-evident,"[34] means that this knowledge which is implanted in us is there "only in the general sense, or 'in a confused manner.'. . . But this, Aquinas says, is not straightforward knowledge of the existence of God, just as to know that someone is coming is not the same as to know Peter, even though it is Peter who is coming. He is in effect saying that God is known under some general conception, as an ultimate end or as the first and most

---

32 "For the precise question being raised is what is the cause of its being conceived"; AT VII 103; CSM II, 75.
33 AT VII, 99; CSM II, 72.
34 *Summa Theologiae*, I, Q. 2, art. i.

perfect being . . . but he is not known in terms of the precise concept of his own proper essence."[35] Caterus's comment refers us to *Summa Theologiae*, Art. 2, Q. 2, where St. Thomas says: "Yet from every effect the existence of the cause can be clearly demonstrated, and so we can demonstrate the existence of God from His effects; though from them we cannot know God perfectly as He is in His essence." Accordingly, natural theology, which is an effect of the operations of natural reason, allows us to demonstrate the existence of God, but it is of no avail when it comes to telling us *what* God is or His *quiddity*. Hence the need for the Bible and the revealed theology contained therein. Descartes's proof strikes at the very heart of the Thomistic distinction between Natural and Revealed theology. Here Descartes's anti-Thomism comes to the fore unabashedly: "The whole force of my proof," Descartes writes, "depends on this one fact. For, firstly, this idea contains the essence of God (*in illa idea contientur quid sit Deus*), at least in so far as I am capable of understanding it; and according to the true logic, we must never ask if it is until we first understand what it is" (*de nulla unquam re quaeri debet as sit, nisi prius quid sit intelligatur*). We can reformulate what Descartes says into Scholastic jargon by saying: "we must never ask about the existence of anything until we know its essence,"[36] which is precisely the reversal of St. Thomas's position.)

Let us ask a commonsensical but a necessary question: Why didn't Descartes's proof convince Caterus, who represents a faithful Scholastic position. In the crucial passage from the Third Meditation, where Descartes employs Scholastic terms, he states:

> Undoubtedly, the ideas which represent substances to me amount to something more and, so to speak, contain within themselves more *objective reality* than the ideas which merely represent modes or accidents. Again, the idea that gives me my understanding of a supreme God . . .certainly has in it more *objective reality* than the ideas that represent finite substances.

35   AT VII, 96–97; CSM II, 70.
36   AT VII, 107; CSM II, 78. In quoting here the last sentence I substituted CSM's literal translation provided by the translator in footnote 1 (p. 78) in the main body of the text and after "In other words."

Now it is manifest by natural light that there must be at least as much reality in the efficient and total cause as in the effect of that cause. For where, I ask, could the effect get its reality from, if not from the cause? And how could the cause give it to the effect unless it possessed it? It follows from this both that something cannot arise from nothing, and also that what is more perfect – that is, contains in itself more reality – cannot arise from what is less perfect. And this is transparently true not only in the case of effects which possess what the philosophers call *actual* or *formal* reality, but also in the case of ideas, where one is considering only what they call *objective* reality. A stone, for example, which previously did not exist, cannot begin to exist unless it is produced by something which contains, either *formally* or *eminently,* everything to be found in the stone; similarly, heat cannot be produced in an object which was not previously hot, except by something of at least the same order (degree or kind) of perfection as heat, and so on.

But it is also true that the idea of heat, or of a stone, cannot exist in me unless it is put there by some cause which contains at least as much reality as I conceive to be in the heat or in the stone. For although this cause does not transfer any of its *actual* or *formal* reality to my idea, it should not on that account be supposed that it must be less real. The nature of an idea is such that of itself it requires no *formal* reality except what it derives from my thought, of which it is a mode. But in order for a given idea to contain such *objective* reality, it must surely derive it from some cause which contains at least as much *formal* reality as there is *objective* reality in the idea. For if we suppose that an idea contains something which was not in its cause, it must have got this from nothing; yet the mode of being by which a thing exists *objectively* or *representatively* in the intellect by way of an idea, imperfect though it may be, is certainly not nothing, and so it cannot come from nothing.[37]

Although Descartes's vocabulary is, by his own admission, of Scholastic provenance, he is explicit in making it known that he

---

37   AT VII, 40–41; CSM II, 28–29.

extends their application beyond their traditional usage. The crucial difference between him and his Scholastic predecessors is this: in contradistinction to the Scholastics, Descartes works on the assumption that the world may not exist, and, therefore, the ideas that I have of external objects could not have come from without. Take the example of the stone used by Descartes in the above fragment. For a Scholastic, the idea of a stone came from an actually existing stone, as did the ideas of all other objects. Henceforth, insofar as the Cartesian mind can have ideas, their origin and their content must be different from their Scholastic counterparts. At the very outset Descartes states that an idea does not require "formal" reality, that is, a cause. In other words, for me to have an idea of a stone, for example, I do not have to see an actual stone, which in the Scholastic picture of the world was the cause of this idea. If so, the question arises: how did I happen to have the idea of a stone? Here is the novelty of Descartes's application of the old terms. According to Descartes, the relationship which obtains in the case of cause and effect (in the pre-Cartesian, Aristotelian world), which the philosophers call *eminent* and *formal* reality, obtains also among ideas. To illustrate the traditional, Scholastic usage of *formal* and *eminent* reality, let me quote Scotus, who in his *De esse Dei* writes:

> If the First Being at one and the same time *formally* possessed all causal power, even though the things which it could cause could not be given simultaneous existence, it would be infinite, because – as far as it is concerned – it has power enough to produce an infinite number at once, and the more one can produce simultaneously, the greater the power in intensity. But if the First Being possessed such power in an even more perfect way than if it had it *formally* [as Avicenna, for instance, assumes], its intensive infinity follows *a fortiori*. But the full causal power that each thing may have in itself, the First Being possesses even more perfectly than if it were *formally* present. . . . Also, the First Being, according to Aristotle,[38] contains all the perfections in a more perfect manner than if they were *formally* present, were this latter possible.

38 Scotus most likely has in mind Aristotle's discussion in his *Physics* VIII and *Metaphysics* XII.

The proof of this lies in the fact that the secondary cause closest to the first receives all of its causal perfection exclusively from the first. *Consequently, the First Cause has the whole of this perfection in a more eminent way than the second cause, which possesses it* formally. The consequence is evident, since the first is the total equivocal cause of the second. We can argue the same way regarding the relation of the third cause to the second or first cause. If we take it in relation to the first, we have the proposed conclusion. If we take it in relation to the second, then it follows that the second cause contains the total perfection found *formally* in the third. But as we have shown, the second cause owes this all to the First Cause; therefore, the First Cause must contain the perfection of the third in an even more perfect way than does the second.[39] And the same is true with all the other causes down to the very last. Therefore we conclude that the First Cause contains *eminently* the total causal power of perfection of all the other causes, and this is a way that is even more perfect than if it contained this causality *formally*, were it possible.[40]

Let me quote another passage from Scotus's *De primo principio*, 4.54 (cf. 4.55):

Although the prior first cause contains in a more excellent way the whole perfection of the second in causing, and to that extent surpasses the second which has this perfection only *formally*, still it is more excellent, even as regards causation, to possess it only *eminently*. To state it in universal terms, when the *formal* possession of any perfection adds to the eminent possession of the same, then together they are more excellent than either taken singly.

What Scotus is saying is this: imagine a series of causes, A➤B➤ C➤D, where A is the First Cause. The First Cause contains *eminently* all the perfections that B possesses only *formally*.[41] However, if we consider B to be the "First Cause" with respect to

39 *De primo principio*, 4.54 and 4.55.
40 *De esse Dei, ibid.*, pp. 64–66 (emphasis mine).
41 Note, however, that in addition to *formal* reality, Descartes uses the term "actual" reality, which he uses interchangeably with "formal" reality.

C, then B possesses eminently the perfections that C possesses formally. This scheme can also be illustrated by means of the following example: imagine a series of metal plates A, B, C, D, and so on; add to this illustration a fire which heats plate A. The fire heats plate A, plate A transfers heat onto plate B, which in turn transfers heat onto plate C, and so on. Now, although plate C receives heat from plate B, which possesses heat only formally, B does not possess the heat eminently, because it is not the *eminent* or *per se* source of heat (since it received heat from A) despite the fact that it is the immediate source of heat for C.

In the Third Meditation Descartes also invokes the idea of a stone.[42] "But in order for [an idea of the stone] to contain such *objective* reality, it must surely derive it from some cause which contains at least as much *formal* reality as there is *objective* reality in the idea." So far, so good, one might say. However, given that I did not see a stone, the question arises: how did I acquire an idea of a stone? Let me bring in here again Duns Scotus, who in his *De primo principio* invokes also the example of a stone, in the context of the discussion of Divine understanding. According to Scotus, God's knowledge of a stone is "intuitive" (*Si igitur intellectionem intuitivam habet Deus de lapide*; *De primo principio*, 4.53). And that is how Scotus explains what intuitive knowledge is: God's knowledge of the stone is not caused by the actually existing stone[43]; God knows the stone through His essence (*per quam lapis sic cognoscitur*; *ibid*). Therefore, in God's case, "cognition through a cause" is unnecessary; what is more, it does not add anything to God's knowledge of the actual stone. In Descartes's scheme the knowledge of the external world is posterior to having the ideas of objects in it.[44] Thus if I happen to have an idea of a stone, it must have been transferred into my mind by a being who has the

---

42 Descartes's use of this example may be indicative of his reading of Scotus's *De primo principio*. It was a common practice among philosophers to use the same examples, not to invent new ones (see footnote 19 above, and my *Augustinian-Cartesian Index* (South Bend, Ind: St. Augustine's Press, 2004), pp. 158–61), and it is unlikely that Descartes came up with this example, which is already in Scotus.

43 See also, *De primo principio*, 4.72.

44 For the so called "similarity thesis," see Med. V, AT VII, 63–64; CSM II, 44–45.

(*eminent*) knowledge of the stone, and this idea, which He transferred into my mind, must contain, as Descartes says, "at least as
much [objective] reality as I conceive to be in the stone." Within
the context of his system, Descartes is justified to say that *objective* reality of an idea is not an extraneous label; it is much more:
it contains reality (which he calls *objective*), which is a trademark
representing an external object which was transferred to my mind
not by an actual stone but by God. Looked at from the point of view
of Scotus's considerations, one might say that Cartesian *objective*
reality is the human equivalent of what Scotus terms God's intuitive knowledge – minus the *eminent* reality which is part of God's
knowledge. It would not be incorrect to say that Scotus's *formal*
reality, when applied to Descartes, corresponds to Descartes's
objective reality. The only reason, in my opinion, for Descartes to
retain the term *objective* reality with respect to ideas was the fact
that this term was traditionally used with respect to them.
However, insofar as *formal* reality in Scotus signifies the reality of
objects transferred from the cause which has this reality eminently, Descartes's understanding of *objective* overlaps with Scotus's
understanding of *formal*.

Why did Descartes need to modify the meaning of Scholastic
terms? The answer imposes itself: in a philosophical system in
which objects do not transfer their images through the senses,
ideas, first, are not pictures of things seen, and therefore their content must be grasped through understanding.[45] Secondly, the trans-

---

45 Let me quote here Timothy Cronin, who tackles the question of
Descartes's use of objective reality from the point of view of his encounter
with Suarez: "Since the actual material world [for the Scholastics] is
made known to us in sensation, the question whether the material world
actually exists, is never asked. The actual existence of the material world
is a datum given to us in sensation. Totally other is the position of
Descartes, who, since he has established the thinking substance as his
first principle, must be means of ideas within this substance demonstrate
the actuality of all other beings. Thus, the second role within his system
of objective reality of ideas is their employment as the means by which
the actuality of the material world is demonstrated. Suarez never asks the
question with which Descartes begins his Sixth Meditation: "It remains
for me to examine whether things exist." "Objective Reality of Idea in
Human Thought: Descartes and Suarez," *ibid.*, p. 72.

fer of the reality of those objects which the ideas in my mind are the repository required of Descartes to construe a theory of causation between God's mind and the *res cogitans*. In other words, insofar as my mind has ideas of external objects which did not come from them, there must be a path for the transference of ideas from the Divine mind (*eminent* reality) to the human mind (*objective* reality). The similarity thesis expounded by Descartes in the Fifth Meditation, according to which objects are merely similar to ideas that I have of them, supports this claim. It is also consistent with Descartes's claim that God, who transfers those ideas into my mind, is not a deceiver.

Scotus is an unlikely candidate to have contributed to Descartes's theory of *objective* reality, simply because he does not employ this term. However, it appears that his considerations[46] concerning the relationship between *eminent* and *formal* reality, and God's intuitive knowledge could have helped Descartes to develop a theory of the human mind which can know essences of things without the help of the senses.

---

46 Note: right after saying "And this is transparently true not only in the case of effects which possess what the philosophers call *actual* or *formal* reality" (the latter form of reality is used by Scotus, which may mean that Scotus is among the philosophers whom Descartes has in mind), Descartes invokes the example of a stone, which is also used by Scotus.

How to Read the Fourth Meditation: Augustinian Sources of Descartes's Metaphysics[1]

Despite the universal recognition of Descartes's philosophical genius, the commentators of his works have been highly critical of his metaphysics. To Etienne Gilson "the metaphysics of Descartes had largely been a clumsy overhauling of scholastic metaphysics."[2] In *Being and Some Philosophers*, one of the most important books on metaphysics produced in this century, Gilson devoted hardly more than a few pages to Descartes's metaphysics, finding in it "something amateurish."[3] The judgment of Martin Heidegger is no more favorable. In discussing the question of Being, Heidegger writes, "Descartes is always far behind the Schoolmen."[4] The question of whether Descartes's metaphysical sophistication matches that of the Scholastics' – whose metaphysics both to Gilson and Heidegger was a yardstick of philosophical refinement – is, however, additionally obstructed by the fact that Descartes never laid out his metaphysics in a systematic fashion. What we find in the *Meditations*, is a jumble of metaphysical terms. As one of Descartes's recent commentators remarked:

1   This chapter was originally published in *Dionysius* XIX (2001): 167–86. Professors Jean-Luc Marion and Daniel Garber have read an earlier version of this text. I am very grateful for their criticisms and suggestions.
2   *God and Philosophy*, Powell Lectures on Philosophy at Indiana University (New Haven, Conn.: Yale University Press, 1941), p. xiv.
3   *Being and Some Philosophers* (Toronto: Pontifical Institute of Mediaeval Studies, 1952), p. 113.
4   Martin Heidegger, *Being and Time*, translated by John Macquarrie & Edward Robinson (San Francisco: Harper & Row, 1962), p. 120.

Descartes in the *Meditations* never asks nor discusses the question, what is being, or substance, or essence. Nothing approaching a definition is found of these terms. . . . Does he utilize the metaphysical terminology of the tradition unaware of, or unconcerned with, the precision with which its issues and implications had been treated in the tradition? Or does he employ it as an *ad hominem* concession to the regnant scholasticism of the day? In *Discourse* I (para. 2) he introduces the reader to his use of scholastic language by employing the terms "forms or natures," "accidents," "individuals," and "species." . . . We find that in the *Meditations* he uses little or no traditional terminology until in *Meditations* III he addresses himself to the first part of his apologetic intention, the proof that God exists. Abruptly a group of scholastic terms is introduced, scarcely defined and devoid of supporting explanation – "objective reality," "formal or actual reality," "eminent reality." . . . "Essence" is never defined in any Cartesian publication: *what meaning employed by what philosopher of the tradition should we fall back on?*[5]

Particularly irritating is the reading of the Fourth Meditation, in which Descartes is working out the theory of nature and origin of falsity. He uses a number of traditional metaphysical notions without taking the trouble, however, to state precisely the meaning of any of them. Etienne Gilson, who devoted several hundred pages of his *La liberté chez Descartes et la theologie* (1913) to investigating the sources of Descartes's philosophy, unable to precisely pinpoint them, came to the conclusion that "the whole Fourth Meditation is a web of borrowings from the theology of St. Thomas and that of the Oratory. It will not be an exaggeration to say that it contains *nothing* original . . ."[6]

Cartesian scholars by and large have accepted Gilson's conclusion, and no attempt to reconsider it ever since has been undertaken. As a result, Descartes's metaphysics remains in the eyes of

---

5   Richard Kennington, "The 'Teaching of Nature' in Descartes's Soul Doctrine," *The Review of Metaphysics*, vol. 26, 1972, pp. 91–93; emphasis mine.

6   Etienne Gilson, *La liberté chez Descartes et la théologie* (Paris: Félix Alcan, 1913), p. 441; emphasis mine.

Descartes critics a kaleidoscope of different metaphysical traditions. This article is an attempt to reconsider Descartes's metaphysics from the questions of both its sources and its originality in general. While rejecting Gilson's thesis about the kaleidoscopic character of Cartesian metaphysics,[7] I share his view that the

---

7   A discussion of the Scholastic doctrine of error would lead us too far away from Descartes. It will suffice for our present purposes to remark that while, according to the Scholastics, only the *will* to deny or to doubt are *acts* of the will, the *acts* of denying or doubting are acts of the intellect. For Descartes in turn, assuring, denying, and doubting are different acts of will (see *Principles of Philosophy*, I, 32). According to Descartes, who confounds the acts of the will with those of intelligence, the Scholastic theory was contradictory. "Since I understand falsity to be merely a privation of the truth, I am convinced that there would be a total contradiction involved in the intellect's apprehending falsity under the guise of truth; but this would have to be the case if the intellect were ever to determine the will to embrace what is false" (*Fifth Set of Replies* , AT VII, 378; CSM II, 260. Cf. Descartes's letter to Mersenne, end of May 1637; AT I, 366; CSM III, 56).

Let us use several quotations from St. Thomas to illustrate Descartes's disagreement.

(1) "Since the object of the will is the good, or at least the apparent good, the will is never attracted by evil unless it appears to have an aspect of good about it, so that the will never chooses evil except by reason of ignorance or error" (*Quia cum voluntas sit boni vel apparentis boni, nunquam voluntas in malum moveretur nisi id quod non est bonum aliqualiter rationi bonum appararet: et propter hoc voluntas nunquam in malum tenderet, nisi cum aliqua ignorantia vel errore rationis*) (ST, Ia2æ. Q.77, Art. 2, Resp. *St Thomas Aquinas Summa Theologiae*, Latin text and English Translation, Blackfriars edition, vol. 25, p. 165).

(2) "Evil is said to be outside the will in the sense that the will does not desire it under the aspect of evil. However, sometimes a thing which is evil in itself has the appearance of good so that in desiring it the will does desire evil" (*Ad primum ergo dicendum quod malum dicitur esse praeter voluntatem, quia voluntas non tendit in ipsum sub ratione mali. Sed qui aliquod malum est apparens bonum, ideo voluntas aliquando appetit aliquod malum*) (ST, I2æ. Q.74, Art. 2. *Ibid.*, vol. 25, p. 165).

(3) "When sin occurs in human behavior it comes either from a defect of intellect, e.g., as when one sins from ignorance; or from a defect of the sense appetite, e.g., as when one sins by reason of emotional disturbance; or from a defect of the will which is nothing but an inherent lack of order. Lack of order can be ascribed to the human will when it loves a lesser good too much." (*Peccatum igitur in humanis actibus contingit quandoque, sicut ex defectu intellectus, puta cum aliquis per*

theology of the Oratory had a considerable impact on the development of Descartes's metaphysics. However, unlike Gilson, I believe that Descartes borrowed the *whole* metaphysics of the Fourth Meditation *directly* from the writings of St. Augustine. Once St. Augustine is established as the primary source for the Fourth Meditation, thus without saving Descartes from the accusation of the lack of originality, we can at least save Descartes from the accusation of careless and arbitrary borrowings.

I

Before examining St. Augustine's writings in light of Descartes's metaphysics in the Fourth Meditation, let us make a few preliminary remarks. Unlike God who on account of His absolute omnipotence enjoys the "freedom of indifference," man, according to Descartes, finds all the norms of the true and the good already established by God. Hence Descartes infers that man's freedom lies in directing his judgments in accordance with these norms and pursuing a clearly known good.[8] In the Fourth Meditation – in which Descartes's considerations about the nature of truth and falsity are intricately linked with those on the nature of human freedom – Descartes remarks that freedom of indifference (*libertas indifferentia*), which is the *essence* of Divine freedom, in man is "the lowest degree of freedom" (*infimus gradus libertatis*),[9] and testifies only to "a *defect* in cognition, or to some *negation*" (*tantummodo in cogitatione defectum, sive negationem quandam, testatur*). When the will has no more reason to incline itself in one direction rather than another, it becomes *indifferent* and "it easily turns aside from what is true and good, and this is the source of my error and sin."[10]

Whence error?

---

ignoratiam peccat, et ex defectu appetitus sensitivi, sicut cum aliquis ex passione peccat, ita etiam ex defectu voluntatis, qui est inordinatio ipsius. Est autem voluntas inordinata, quando minus bonum magis amat) (ST, I2æ. Q. 78, Art. 1. *Ibid.*, vol. 25, p. 190–91. Cf. *Ibid.*, Arts. 78, 3; 74, 8; 76, 4; 75, 2; 8, 1).

8   AT VII, 432–33; CSM II, 291–92.

9   AT VII, 58; CSM II, 40. Cf. Leibniz, *Theodicée*, 33–53.

10   AT VII, 58; CSM II, 40–41.

In this *incorrect* use of the *liberum arbitrium* is to be found that *privation* which constitutes the essence of error. The privation, I say, lies in the operation of [the will] itself *in so far as it proceeds from me*, but not in the faculty of will [*the liberum arbitrium*] which I received from God, nor even in its operation, in so far as it depends on Him.[11]

The crucial term in the above passage is the personal pronoun *me* – *privatio . . . quatenus a me procedit; privation . . . in so far as it proceeds from me* – the meaning of which Descartes explains in the following way:

> I find that I possess not only a real and positive idea of God, or of a being that is supremely perfect (*entis summe perfecti*), but also what may be described as a negative idea of nothingness (*nihili . . . negativam quandam ideam mihi obvervari*), or of that which is farthest removed from all perfection. I realize that I am, as it were, a middle something between God and nothingness, or between the highest being and nonbeing (*tanquam medium quid inter Deum & nihil, sive inter summum ens & non ens ita esse constitutum*): my nature is such that in so far as I was created by the highest being, there is surely nothing in me to enable me to go wrong or lead me astray; but in so far as I also participate in nothingness or non-being, that is, in so far as I am not myself the highest being himself (*sed quatenus etiam quodammodo de nihilo, sive de non ente, participio, hoc est quatenus non sum ipse summum ens*) and am lacking in countless respects, it is no wonder that I would be deceived.[12]

Let us briefly reiterate the main points of Descartes's account. (1) In creating man, God endowed him with *liberum arbitrium*. (2) Error is not something positive or real (*non esse quid reale*), that is, it does not require a positive force on the part of God, but rather it is only a lack, a privation (*privatio*) or a defect (*tantummodo esse defectum*). 3) It arises from the incorrect use of the *liberum arbitrium*. To explain how this incorrect use of the *liberum arbitrium* comes about – and this is the real crux of Descartes's

11 AT VII, 60; CSM II, 41.
12 AT VII, 54; CSM II, 38.

argument in the Fourth Meditation, although it is seldom discussed in Cartesian literature[13] – Descartes draws on the *difference* between the respective natures of God and man. While God is "the most perfect being" (*ens summe perfectum*) or "the highest being" (*summum ens*), man is "a middle something" (*tanquam medium*) between God and nothing, or, as Descartes puts it in yet another way, between the *highest being* and *non-being* (*medium quid inter Deum et nihil, sive inter summum ens & non ens ita esse constitutum*). Furthermore, insofar as man *participates* in nothingness (*nihil*) or in non-being (*non ens*) he is subject to error.

Although Descartes's only goal in this passage is to explain the meaning of the single personal pronoun *me*, he resorts to a battery of metaphysical terms: "being" and "non-being," "privation" and "negation," "participation," "highest Being." None of these terms, strangely enough, he explains. Descartes says neither what *privation* or *negation* are[14] (we are told that error is *privation* but we are not told a privation of *what*); nor in what way man "participates" in non-being; nor what it means that God is the "highest being;" and, last but not least, how the fact that man is not the "highest being" (*summum ens*) or the "most perfect Being" (*Ens summe perfectum*) accounts for man's being subject to deception.

The statement, "in so far as I am not God, it is not very surprising that I would be deceived," is far from clear. If we take it at face value, it explains literally nothing, or it yields a tautology: if to be infallible means to be perfect, and only the highest being is perfect, and man is not the highest being, therefore *non mirum est* that man is subject to deception. Only with the greatest of difficulty can we ascribe to Descartes's statement any explanatory power. Needless to say, if that is what Descartes is really saying, the argument instead of vindicating God's goodness and omnipotence leads

13 See Etienne Gilson, *La liberté chez Descartes*, pp. 211–35.

14 Cf. *Principles of Philosophy*, I, 31, and Descartes's letter to Regius, May 24, 164 (AT III, 65). According to L. J. Beck (*The Metaphysics of Descartes: A Study of the Meditations* [Westport, Conn.: Greenwood Press, 1979 ed., p. 205, footnote 1), Descartes is using here "privation" in Aristotle's sense of *steresis* (loss, deprivation). Cf. the quotation from Suarez cited by Gilson in his *Index Scholastico-Cartesien* (p. 245): "nam privatio dicit carentiam in subjecto apto nato."

Descartes back to the problem which he attempted to overcome, namely, that God might be responsible for error: either God has not conferred on man something which could keep him from deception,[15] in which case His benevolence is at stake; or God could not create human nature in such a way that man could avoid error, in which case His omnipotence is at stake.

We should not, however, suspect Descartes of committing such an apparent logical blunder. If his account raises problems, these concern, first and foremost, his understanding of God. We are told that God is the *most perfect Being* (*Ens summe perfectum*), but what exactly is this *Ens summe perfectum*? Is the *Ens summe perfectum* (the most perfect Being) the same as *summum ens* (the highest Being; another expression used in the same passage), or, perhaps, *Ens summe perfectum* means just *Ens* (*Being*)? But if so, why is Descartes using the expression *Ens summe perfectum* (the most perfect Being) or *summum ens* (the highest Being) rather than simply *Ens* (Being)? Possibly, to suggest another line of interpretation, the two terms – the highest Being and the most perfect Being – should be taken to mean a Being (*Ens*) which possesses certain attributes which man does not possess. The two definitions of God that Descartes offers in the Third Meditation might support such an interpretation.

The first reads: "a God sovereign, eternal, infinite, immutable, all knowing, all powerful, and universal creator of all things" (*illa [idea] per quam summum aliquem Deum, aeternum, infinitum, omniscium, omnipotentem, rerumque omnium, quae praeter ipsum sunt creatorem intelligo*).[16]

The second reads: "By the name God I understand a substance infinite, eternal, immutable, all knowing, all powerful, and by which I myself and all other things (if it is true that any such exist) have been created and produced (*Dei nomine intelligo substantiam quandam infinitam, independentem, summe intelligentem, summe potentem, et a qua tum ego ipse, tum aliud omne si quid aliud extat, quodcumque extat, est creatum*).[17]

15 In a short passage in the Fourth Meditation Descartes considers such a possibility: AT VII 61; CSM II, 42.

16 AT VII, 40; CSM II, 28.

17 AT VII, 45; CSM II, 31.

We could interpret the expression *Ens summe perfectum* to imply the existence of a hierarchy of "beings" or "substances" of which God is the most perfect. The difference between the highest Being (God) and lesser beings (like man) would lie in that the highest Being possesses certain attributes (infinity, eternity, etc.), which the latter do not possess. By placing God on the top of the ladder of beings, the equation between God as *Ens* in the Fourth Meditation and God as *Substantia* in the Third Meditation is rather unproblematic: God as *Substantia* would be the highest Being in the sense of being a unique bearer of certain attributes. Thus, the problem of the mutual translatability of these two definitions of God as "Being" and "Substance" disappears.[18]

This reading is not free of difficulties, however. Even if God – as the only bearer of some attributes – is, so to speak, the only genus of His species, He would be the *highest* being among other *beings*. Accordingly, God is a being that possesses certain attributes which man does not – but both God and man are essentially *beings*. The problem with this interpretation is that it makes the difference between God and other beings "quantitative" rather than "qualitative." Descartes could defend himself against this accusation by saying that God is a unique being not only because He possesses certain attributes which other beings do not possess, but because *no* other beings can possess them. Be that as it may, this argument is exposed to a simple objection: as it is in the nature of man not to be, say, eternal or omnipotent, etc., it is not in the nature of God to possess the attributes which are proper for "lower" beings; the fact that God is the only such a being who is eternal, immutable, etc., whereas there are many beings such as man, does not matter since both man and God are essentially *beings*. Thus God's "uniqueness" in the sense that only He is, e.g., immutable, eternal, etc. is insufficient to account for God's being the *highest* Being.

---

18 For a very instructive and erudite discussion of different problems with Descartes's definition of God see Jean-Luc Marion, "The Essential Incoherence of Descartes's Definition of Divinity," in Amélie Oksenberg Rorty (ed.), *Essays on Descartes' Meditations* (Berkeley: University of California Press, 1986), pp. 297–338.

II

It needs to be noted, however, that the problem which we just addressed is not peculiar to Descartes's account, but has always been one of the most essential questions of Christian metaphysics and Descartes's is only one more expression of the perennial problem of finding an adequate definition of Being. The term *Ens* or *Essentia* has a long history and was coined because the term *substantia* – which implicates that it "underlies" attributes, while God's attributes are not accidents properly speaking – was always thought to be insufficient for defining God's essence. To St. Augustine, who to a large extent is the true author of the definition of God as *Essentia*, "God is *improperly* called substance and better usage requires that He be understood as *essence*, which He is truly and properly called." To this St. Augustine adds: "perhaps God alone should be called essence. For He alone truly is immutable."[19] In other words, only that which is immutable really *is*, and only that which *is* can be properly called *Essentia*. Thus God as *Essentia* or *Ens* (the latter term, used by Descartes, was a

19 *De Trinitate*, VII, 4–5; 9–10: "For just as essence receives its name from being [esse], so substance is derived from subsisting. But it is absurd to give a relative meaning to the word substance, for everything subsists in respect to itself; how much more God? If, indeed, it is fitting to speak of God as subsisting! For to subsist is rightly applied to those things to which the qualities, which need another being in order to be able to be, cling for support, as the color or form of the body. . . . Therefore, things that are changeable and not simple are properly called substances. But if God subsists, so that He may be properly called a substance, then there is something in Him as it were in a subject, and He is no longer simple; His being, accordingly, would not be one and the same with the other qualities that are predicated of Him in respect to Himself, as for example, to be great, omnipotent, good, and any other attributes of this kind that are not unfittingly said of God. But it is wrong to assert that God subsists and is the subject of His own goodness, and that goodness is not a substance, or rather not an essence, that God Himself is not His own goodness, and that it inheres in Him as in its subject. It is, therefore, obvious that God is improperly called a substance. The more usual name is essence, which He is truly and properly called, so that perhaps God alone should be called essence. For He is truly alone, because He is unchangeable." Cited after Vernon Bourke, *Augustine's View of Reality* (Philadelphia: Villanova University, 1963), pp. 91–92. Cf. *De Trinitate*, VII, 5, 10; Cf. *Enar. in Ps.* CXXI, 3, 6; *De Trinitate*, VII, 4, 7–8. Bourke's little book contains an excellent essay on St. Augustine's metaphysics.

Scholastic invention unknown to St. Augustine[20]) signifies, first and foremost, that which *is* or *exists*. Thus, God's essence is the act of existence.

Since only in God essence and existence are one, Descartes's expression *Ens summe perfectum* might suggest that the *summe perfectum* (the most perfect) adds something to *Ens* (Being), implying, therefore, that there are either grades of existence or that existence in equal degree belongs to the essence of creatures as it does to God, but then, the creatures would exist necessarily as God does. Another complication with the definition of God as *ens summe perfectum* is that the very notion of the "higher" and the "lower," "more perfect" and "less perfect," presupposes a scale, a measurement by means of which one could estimate the position of a given being on the ladder of beings. But such a measurement would need to be independent of God. Descartes's doctrine of the eternal truths, according to which God is the creator of all possible norms, and subject to none (otherwise, as Descartes says, God would be like a Jupiter subject to the Fates or the Styx), precludes the possibility of the existence of such a scale. Thus the "quantitative" interpretation runs counter both to the traditional understanding of *Ens* as *existence*, which Descartes accepted,[21] and to his own doctrine of divine omnipotence which he formulated as the doctrine of the eternal truths. Accordingly, the *summe perfectum* is, it seems, merely a superfluous addition to *Ens*, and we should therefore take Descartes's *Ens summe perfectum* to mean a unique being not only in the sense that God possesses certain attributes which only the *highest being* can possess, but in the sense that only God is *Ens*, properly speaking. However, to say this implies that man can be called *ens* only "improperly" or conditionally.

Before we discuss this problem, let us first ask, what is it about

20 On the development of this notion see Etienne Gilson, "Notes sur le vocabulaire de l'être," *Medieval Studies*, VII, (1946), 150–158. Cf. J. Owens, *Being in the Aristotelian Metaphysics* (Toronto: Pontifical Institute of Medieval Studies, 1951), pp. 65–74.

21 In the Fifth Meditation (AT VII, 68; CSM II, 47) Descartes states: "First of all, there is the fact that, apart from God, there is nothing else of which I am capable of thinking such that existence [necessarily – reads the French version] belongs to its essence."

the idea of God as *Being* (*Ens*) that, despite all the difficulties which it raises, made Descartes use it in the Fourth Meditation rather than *Substance* (*Substantia*)? Descartes's goal in the Fourth Meditation is to explain how error comes about. In contradistinction to *Substantia*, which defines God through His attributes, the notion of *Ens* (Being) allows Descartes to construct the notion of non-being which Descartes needs for the interpretation of error as *privation*, and which in turn he needs to explain in what sense error proceeds from *me*. While error as *privation* is unintelligible without knowing what it is privation *of*, the definition of man as a "middle something" between Being and non-being is equally unintelligible without constructing the idea of *non-being*. Descartes's theory of error as privation of being is of course nothing but a projection into the field of epistemology of the well-known Augustinian idea of evil as privation of being. Let us make a short digression here. In "epistemologizing" the Augustinian theory of evil, Descartes, like St. Augustine, can easily exonerate God from the responsibility for man's going wrong. However, in so doing he will inherit all the problems of Augustinian theology. Now the extent to which Cartesian metaphysics is in fact a "secularized" version of Christian theology, Descartes must find room in his purely "rational" philosophy for the Christian notion of Original Sin.[22]

22 The question of Original Sin has been always a problem for those Cartesian scholars who insist on the essentially Christian character of Descartes's philosophy. In a recent article on Descartes's theory of error Donald A. Cress makes the following remark:

> The Fourth Meditation made full use of virtually every major theme in Augustine's theodicy with the important exception of [Original] sin. . . . It is highly problematic how one is to attempt a complete and coherent theodicy by appropriating all of the other components of Augustine's theodicy while refraining for methodological reasons from any mention of one: [Original] sin. . . . The real question is, of course, not whether Descartes was a consistent and faithful Augustinian, but whether his partial Augustinism is fully up to the task of providing a coherent and complete explanation of the origin of falsity. (Donald A. Cress "Truth, Error, and the Order of Reasons," *Reason, Will, and Sensation in Descartes' Metaphysics*, ed. by John Cottingham [Oxford: Clarendon Press, 1994], pp. 152–53.)

Up to this point Descartes's theological-epistemology is a description of the formal conditions, or nature, of error. What needs to be further explained is the cause of error: that is, *why*.

To be sure, nowhere in Descartes's entire philosophical *corpus* shall one find an explicit reference to Original Sin as an explanation of the epistemological problems addressed in the *Meditations*. Yet Original Sin insofar as it is defined in Christian tradition as the "rebellion of the flesh against the spiritual nature" is not absent from Descartes's philosophy. Several decades ago Henri Gouhier (and recently Daniel Garber, as the only English speaking Descartes commentator) put forth a convincing claim that Descartes's account of infancy is the secularized counterpart of the Christian idea of Original Sin. "Why is infancy a species of Original Sin in the order of cognition? Because it is the period in our lives in which our appetites govern us. The spirit of a child is taken up by that which it senses and its first judgments are dictated by the sensations without the control of the intellect." (Gouhier, "Le refus du symbolisme dans l'humanisme Cartésien," *Archivo di Filosofia* [1958], p. 71. See also his "La résistance au vrai et le problème cartésien d'une philosophie sans rhétorique," in, *Atti Congresso internationale di studi umanistici, Venezia, 1954* [Roma: Fratelli Bocca Editori, 1955], pp. 85–97. Cf. Daniel Garber, "*Semel in vita*: The Scientific Background to Descartes' *Meditations*," ed. by E. Rorty, *Essays on Descartes' Meditations* [Berkeley: California University Press], pp. 89–108). It needs to be borne in mind that maturity to Descartes is not a biological category; rather, it is a philosophical postulate which consists in "lay[ing] aside all our preconceived opinions. . . we must take the greatest care not to put our trust in any of the opinions accepted by us in the past until we have first scrutinized them afresh and confirmed their truth" (*Principles of Philosophy* I, 75; AT VIIIA, 38; CSM I, 221). "Detach mind from the senses" (*abducere mentem a sensibus*) sounds Descartes's famous slogan. "What this is all about," Gouhier writes, "is not only the Platonic conflict which the allegory of the Cave illustrates, that is a conflict of intelligence in quest for the intelligibles, a conflict which the soul's union with the body hinders in the sensible world: it concerns the conflict between intelligence in quest for the intelligible and pseudo-intelligence swelled in the pseudo-intelligibles. Of course, this pseudo-intelligence developed itself in favor of the union of soul and body. But for Plato this union is a sign of the fall, the soul is no longer in itself, its body is its prison; for Descartes this union is in conformity with the order of nature and these are the early years of this union which condemn the soul for imprisonment. Here and there is the scandal of the human condition. In the eyes of Plato man begins with the sensible world, in the eyes of Descartes man begins with being an infant. . . . The mission of [Descartes'] philosophy is to substitute man with infant. . . . it is not history which assures the passage from infancy to adult age, but philosophy insofar as it is opposed history. . . . The point is to get

man goes wrong. Descartes's discussion is very scanty and in fact does not go much beyond the two passages we quoted earlier: the absence of clear and distinct ideas causes the will's "indifference," and then it "turns itself aside from truth and good." This is essentially all Descartes has to say. The lack of an extensive discussion makes the Fourth Meditation almost unintelligible, to the point that Descartes's most fundamental question – whence error and how does it come about? – seems to be hanging in the air. Gilson's conclusion about the "kaleidoscopic character" of Descartes's theory of error coupled with the almost complete absence of studies of the Fourth Meditation[23] indeed implies that Descartes had no coherent explanation of the origin of error. Tempting as this explanation seems to be, it is completely incredible.

III

On 21 April 1641, Descartes wrote to his friend Mersenne:

> I wrote [in the Fourth Meditation] that indifference in our case is rather a defect than a perfection of freedom; but it does not follow that the same is the case with God. Nevertheless, I do not know that it is 'an article of faith' to believe hat he is indifferent, and I feel confident that Father Gibieuf will defend my position well on this matter; for *I wrote nothing, which is not in accord with what he said in his book* De libertate.[24]

rid of 'the old man,' who in the Cartesian vision of the universe is nothing but an aged infant." (Gouhier, "La résistance au vrai et le problème cartésien d'une philosophie sans rhétorique," *ibid.*, p. 89–90).

23   In the most recent study of the *Meditations, Descartes: An Analytical and Historical Introduction* (Oxford: Oxford University Press, 1993) by Georges Dicker, which aspires to be a systematic exposition of the *Meditations*, the Fourth Meditation is completely left out. However, when the metaphysics of the Fourth Meditation is discussed, especially among English speaking commentators, it is often full of errors. L. J. Beck, in his very good and interesting study of the Meditations (*The Metaphysics of Descartes: A Study of the Meditations* [Westport, Conn.: Greenwood Press, Publishers, 1979 ed.], p. 208), in discussing the metaphysics of the Fourth Meditation states "The natural tendency of the will is towards the 'good' and the 'true.'" This claim is consistent neither with theological doctrines in the seventeenth century nor with Descartes's own statements.

24   To Mersenne, 21 April 1641 (AT III, 360; CSMK III, 179; emphasis Z.J.).

In another letter to Mersenne, written two months later (June 23 1641), Descartes states, "as for what I wrote about liberty [in the Fourth Meditation], it conforms to that which Reverend Father Gibieuf wrote before me, and I do not think that there is anything to which he could object."[25]

An extensive discussion about the contents of Gibieuf's *De Libertate Dei et Creaturae* (1630) would require a long and detailed treatment which would take us too far away from our present topic, but a few remarks need to be made. Much of the contents of Gibieuf's book, and his conception of freedom in particular, is a philosophical elaboration of the theology of St. Augustine. During the theological debates in the first half of the seventeenth century, especially before the publication of Jansenius' *Augustinus* in 1640, Gibieuf became a primary object of attacks by the Jesuit theologians (Annat, Raynauld, Habert, Dola, Colonia, et al.), some of whom (Annat and Habert) played essential role in furthering the condemnation of Jansenius' Augustinian theology of grace in 1653. The extent to which Gibieuf's theory of human liberty is an exposition of St. Augustine's views, it amounted to criticism of the Molinist-Jesuit understanding of freedom as the possibility of freely acting in one direction or another. In religious terms the semi-Pelagian Molinist doctrine meant that even after the Original Sin man does not need God's grace to choose the good and thus is capable of gaining eternal salvation by means of his own natural resources.

Although the battle between the Augustinians and the Molinists was fought primarily on a theological front and concerned almost exclusively religious issues, it could very easily be translated into purely philosophical categories. The philosophical issue that divided the two camps was freedom of the will. According to Molina, freedom is the power to act or not act, or do something or its opposite; this faculty of acting or of doing something or its opposite when all that is required for acting is given is called liberty (*quo modo id liberum dicimus, quod positis requisitis ad agendum in*

25   Letter to Mersenne, 23 June 1641 (AT III, 385–386). Adrien Baillet writes that "La publication du livre de P. Gibieuf, touchent la liberté de Dieu et de la créature, où il eut le plaisir de trouver de quoi autoriser ce qu'il pensait de l'indifférence et du libre arbitre" (*La vie de Monsieur Descartes* [Paris: La Table Ronde, 1946], p. 87.)

potestate ipsius habet agere aut non agere, aut agere hoc aut oppositum; facultasque illa agendi et non agendi aut agendi hoc aut oppositum positis omnibus requisitis ad agendum appellatur libertas).[26] The Jesuit-Molinist conception of freedom does not presuppose a special metaphysics of good and evil, right or wrong, truth or falsity; there is nothing in it which would not allow us to conceive of freedom as the pursuit of error rather than truth, or evil rather than good. The position of the Molinists entailed, even if they never spelled it out, that in making a wrong choice man also asserts his freedom. From this followed that if we are capable of doing good out of our own resources (and we are since, as the Molinists maintained, God's grace, even if necessary, is distributed equally), we can also be *indifferent* with respect to the choice between good and evil, right and wrong, or truth and falsity.

Gibieuf's position is on the opposite pole. The question which he raises in *De Libertate Dei* concerns whether the liberty of indifference in man is absolute, or, in other words, whether it belongs to the essence of human freedom (*Hic duae quaestiones emergunt: una, utrum indifferentia libertatis sit indifferentia absoluta ad agendum & non agendum.*[27]) In addressing this question, Gibieuf states that the liberty of indifference of the will is only "conditional and tempered" by its end (*Dico I. Indifferentia quae spectat ad liberum arbitrium creaturae, non est indifferentia absoluta ad agendum & non agendum, sed indifferentia conditionata & temperata per respectum ad finem . . . .*[28]) (This is the exact same argument Descartes will use in the Fourth Meditation eleven years later.) Gibieuf concludes his argument – and here he is repeating St. Augustine verbatim – that the more man becomes subject to God's will the more free he is.

Jansenius, who served as an examiner of Gibieuf's work, despite some reservations, found the ' Oratorian's criticism of the freedom of indifference to be the most valuable part of *De Libertate Dei.* "The true liberty of the *liberum arbitrium* known by the

26   Molina, *De Scientia Dei*, published in *Beiträge Zur Geschichte Der Philosophie Und Theologie Des Mittelalters*, Band XXXII (Münster: Aschendorffschen, 1935), p. 207.

27   *De Libertate*, p. 68.

28   *De Libertate*, p. 68–69.

ancient authors," reads Jansenius' approbation, "does not consist in this philosophical indifference to act as it is commonly proclaimed (*quae vulgo praedicatur*). This book demonstrates this with numerous and solid reasons, and it refutes the defenders of contrary opinions."[29] Jansenius' *Augustinus* contains much more severe and elaborate criticism of the freedom of indifference than Gibieuf's work, and there seems to be very little in *De Libertate Dei* as far as the freedom of indifference is concerned which cannot be found in *Augustinus*. However, before the publication of *Augustinus*, which is a strictly theological work, *De Libertate Dei* was the first, and the most important, book to take an open stance against the increasingly powerful partisans of the freedom of indifference.

Descartes's statements on freedom are is in perfect conformity with the Augustinian doctrine of freedom understood as the opposite not of necessity but of compulsion:[30] "in order to be free, there is no need for me to be inclined both ways; on the contrary, the more I incline in one direction – either because I clearly understand that reasons of truth and goodness point that way, or because of a divinely produced disposition [i.e., grace] of my inmost

29 The full text of the approbation reads: "Veram arbitrii Libertatem antiquis Scriptoribus notam, non esse sitam in illa Philosophica indifferentia agendi, quae vulgo praedicatur, multis praeclaris et solidis rationibus hic liber astruit et adversae opinionis defensores confutat. Et quia non modo eruditionem, sed etiam pietatem Auctoris sui testamentum fecit, et Lectoris provocat, dum animum creaturarum visco et nexibus expediendum docet, ut asseratur in libertatem gloriae filiorum Dei; merito omne tulisse punctum dici potest: quia Dei simul et hominis consuluit dignitati" Cornelius Iansenius, S., Thologiae Doctor ac Professor Ordinarius, In Universitate Louvanevsi (13 December 1629). Quoted after Jean Orcibal in *Les origines du Jansénisme*. Vol. I. *Correspondance de Jansénius*, p. 456.

30 AT VII, 58; CSM II, 40. A. Boyce Gibson rightly remarks that "by his deliberate and almost unnecessary allusion to 'divine grace,' and by his use of the technical term, 'liberty of indifference,' which he could easily have avoided, Descartes here ranges himself with one of the parties to the bitterest of the contemporary theological controversies." *The Philosophy of Descartes* (London: Methuem & Co. LTD, 1932), p. 333. Gibson is right but for the wrong reasons. He is referring to the Jansenist movement that did not exist in 1641. Before 1640 it was primarily the Oratorian Fathers who constituted the most influential Augustinian group in France.

thoughts – the freer is my choice. . . . divine grace. . . [does not] diminish freedom, [but] increas[es] and strenghten[s] it." What explains the incompleteness of Descartes's account of the will and the theory of being in the Fourth Meditation is, in my opinion, the fact that he was all too well aware that his account was to a large degree an exposition of Augustinian theology.[31] An open adherence

31   Let us use several questions from Descartes's writings to support our claim: "The will of a thinking thing is drawn voluntarily and freely (for this is the essence of will), but nevertheless *inevitably*, towards a clearly known good" (emphasis mine. Cf. AT VII, 58–59; CSM II, 41). "I can see, however, that God could easily have brought it about that without losing [freedom], and despite the limitations in my knowledge, I should nonetheless never make a mistake. He could, for example, have endowed my intellect with a clear and distinct perception of everything about which I was ever going to deliberate" (AT VII, 61; CSM II, 42). To be sure, there are other places in Descartes's writings, especially those written in 1644, in which Descartes seems to endow will with certain degree of autonomy with respect to the choice between good and evil, which, I believe, is nothing more than a concession for the benefit of the Molinists, who by 1644, that is, by the time of the publication of the *Principles of the Philosophy* and the letters to Mesland, were starting to take the upper hand and in 1653 carried out the condemnation of the Augustine's teaching precisely on this point (the so-called "Five Propositions"; see, e.g., Leszek Kolakowski, *God Owes Us Nothing* [Chicago: The University of Chicago Press, 1995], Part I). However, the core of Cartesian doctrine of freedom of the will remains essentially Augustinian. AT VII, 57; CSM II, 40.

On the condemned propositions, see Antoine Arnauld, "Quinque Propositiones ab Innocentio X Damnatae, et Propositiones Jansenii Yprensis Episcopi, Damnatis Contrariae," in *Œuvres de Messire Antoine Arnauld*, vol. XIX, Paris, 1967. Cf. "Argument du P. Annat," *ibid.*, and "Relation Abrégé sur le sujet des cinq Propositions condamnées par la Constitution du Pape Innocent X," *ibid.*

It needs to be remarked, however, that there are places in the Fourth Meditation, which sound semi-Pelagian, i.e., Molinist. The whole Cartesian definition of free will reads: "[T]he will [or freedom of choice] simply consists in our ability to do or not to do something (that is, to affirm or deny, to pursue or avoid); or *rather*, it consists simply in the fact that when the intellect puts something forward for affirmation or denial or for pursuit or avoidance, our inclinations are such that we do not feel we are determined by any external force" (emphasis mine). This definition comprises two incompatible claims. According to the first part, freedom consists in having a choice between two alternatives. According to the second part, freedom consists in being necessitated to follow one

to the Augustinian theory of freedom could bring on him the wrath of the Molinists, as it had in the case of Gibieuf in the 1630s, and consequently could jeopardize the chances of receiving the approbation for his *Meditations*.[32]

IV

Let us now have a closer look at the major premises of St. Augustine's theology and, next, contrast them with the contents of the Fourth Meditation. St. Augustine begins with the observation that the bodies that constitute the material world change: nothing remains unchanged even for a short time (*in eo nihil manet, nihil vel parvo spatio temporis habet eodem modo*).[33] Physical objects change not only in space but also in time (*Omne autem quod movetur per locum, non potest nisi et per tempus simul moveri*).[34] What causes this change? It would seem that it is matter (*mutabilitas enim rerum mutabilium ipsa capax est formarum omnium, in quas mutantur res mutabiles*).[35] But change

alternative. While the first part is in conformity with the Molinist-Jesuit definition of freedom, the second conforms to the Augustinian understanding of liberty as the pursuit of good only.

    Theological background of Descartes's doctrine of Divine and human freedoms, especially their relations vis-à-vis Molinism, is discussed by Romano Amerio, "Arbitrarismo Divino, Libertà Umana e Implicanze Teologiche Nella Dottrina Di Cartesio," *CARTESIO: Nel Terzo Centenario Del Discorso Del Metodo*, Milano, 1937.

32 It was assumed until recently that the approbation of the Sorbonne for the *Meditations* was never granted. Recently, J.-R. Armogathe convincingly argued on the basis of existing documents that the *Meditations* did receive the approbation. (See his "L'Aprobation des Meditationes par la Faculté de Theologie de Paris (1641)," *Archives de Philosophie*, Bulletin Cartésien, XXI, 57, 1994 (1), pp. 1–3. See also Francis Ferrier's remarks on the same question. *La pensée philosophique du Père Guillaume Gibieuf*, [Lille: Atelier Reproduction de Thèses, 1976], vol. I, p. 125). Four men served as the examiners of the *Meditations*: Chastelain, Potier, Hallier, and Cornet. The hostile attitude of the latter two toward Jansenism is well known. There is very little or almost no information about the other two.

33 *De Ordine*, II, xix, 50 (PL XXXII, 1018).

34 *De Genesi ad litteram*, VIII, xx, 39 (PL XXXIV, 388).

35 *Confessions*, XII, vi, 6 (PL XXXII, 828). Cf. *Confessions*, XII, viii, 8; (PL XXXII, 829); *De vera religione*, c. xviii, 35–36 (PL XXXIV, 137); *De*

also affects souls that are immaterial (*clarum est eam esse muta-bilem*).[36] Thus one cannot account for change by mere reference to matter or mere time, though time and matter or only time are necessary conditions for change. The mutability, however, is a result of something much more fundamental: there was a "time" when what is mutable was *not*, before God created the world. Because God created the world not out of His being (which is impossible since then the world would always have been) but *ex nihilo*,[37] therefore everything must be changeable. Whatever was *created* is by definition mutable (*solus ipse incommutabilis, omnia quae fecit, quia ex nihilo fecit, mutabila sunt*).[38]

In contrast to creation, God is not subject to change, and, therefore, only He can properly be said *to be* (*Id enim vere est, quod incommutabiliter manet*).[39] "It is obvious that God is improperly called substance, and better usage requires that He be understood as essence, which He is truly and properly called: and thus, perhaps *God alone should be called essence. For He alone truly is, since He is immutable.*"[40] This is probably the strongest statement in St. Augustine to the effect that in God *essence* – which, as he says elsewhere, is derived from "what it is to be" (*ab eo quod est esse*)[41] – is *existence*.

If God is the pure act of existence, in what sense can the creatures be said *to be*? It would seem that St. Augustine's definition of God as that which *Is* (*Vere enim ipse est, quia incommutabilis est; omnis enim mutatio facit non esse quod erat*)[42] does not leave room for anything other than God Himself to be called *essentia*. And yet, despite St. Augustine's unequivocal statement to the effect

Genesi liber imperfectus, c. xii 36 (PL XXXIV, 235); *De Genesi ad litteram libri duodecim*, II, xiv, 28 (PL XXXIV, 274–75).

36   *De vera religione*, c. xxx, 54 (PL, XXXIV, 140). Cf. also *De immortalitate animae*, c. v, 7 (PL XXXII, 1025).

37   *De Civitate Dei*, XII, 1.

38   *De natura boni*, I, i (PL XXXII, 811).

39   *Confessions*, VII, 11. 17 (PL XXXII, 742). Cf. *De vera religione*, 18. 35 (PL XXXIV, 137).

40   *De Trinitate*, VII, 5, 10. Cf. *Enar. in Ps.* PL CXXI, 3, 6, also *De Trinitate*, VII, 4, 7–8.

41   *De Trinitate*, V, 2, 3.

42   *De natura boni*, 19 (PL XLII, 557).

that only God is *ousia* or *essentia*[43] (*fortasse solum Deum dici
oporteat essentiam*), he does not restrict the term *essentia* to God
alone. Although in contrast to God creation contains an element of
change, it contains, however, a principle of permanence[44] without
which it would inevitably perish (*nisi permaneret, incommutabilis, nulla mutabilis natura remaneret*).[45] In creating the
world, God imposed on creation three principles: *measure, form,*
and *order* (*modus, species, ordo*): "Since measure determines the
proportions of each thing, number furnishes each thing with its
species, and weight draws each thing to rest and stability, He is
these things firstly, truly, and uniquely, who sets bounds to all,
forms all, and orders all."[46] Insofar as every created thing contains

43 *De Trinitate*, VII, 5. 10 (PL XLII, 942): "Est tamen sine dubitatione sub-
    stantia, vel, si melius hoc appellatur, essentia quam Graeci ousiam vocant
    . . . Aliae quae dicuntur essentiae sive substantiae, capiunt accidentia,
    quibus in eis fiat vel magna vel quantacumque mutatio: Deum autem aliq-
    uid ejusmodi accidere non potest; et ideo sola est incommutabilis sub-
    stantia vel essentia, qui Deus est" (*Ibid.*, V, 2. 3). In *De Civitate Dei*, XII,
    2 St. Augustine states: "The quickest and easiest way for anyone to divest
    himself of that erroneous and blasphemous notion is to understand clear-
    ly what God said by the mouth of his angel when sending Moses to the
    children of Israel: God said, 'I am HE WHO IS' [Exodus 3, 14]. For God is
    existence in a supreme degree – he supremely is – and he is therefore
    immutable. Hence he gave existence to the creatures he made out of
    nothing; but it was not his own supreme existence. To some he gave exis-
    tence in a higher degree, to some in a lower, and thus he arranged a scale
    of existences of various natures. Now 'existence' (*essentia*) is derived
    from the verb 'to be' or 'to exist' (*esse*), in the same way as 'wisdom' (*sapi-
    entia*) from the verb 'to be wise' (*sapere*). It is a new word, not employed
    by ancient writers, but it has come into general use in modern times to
    supply the need for a Latin word to express what the Greeks call *ousia*,
    of which *essentia* is a literal translation. Thus the highest existence, from
    which all things that are derive their existence, the only contrary nature
    is the non-existent. Non-existence is obviously contrary to the existent. It
    follows that no existence is contrary to God, that is to the supreme exis-
    tence and the author of all existence whatsoever."
44 "Deus cujus legibus in aevo stantibus, motus instbilis rerum mutabilium
    perturbatus esse non sinitur, frenisque circumeuntium saeculorum sem-
    per ad similitudinem stabilitatis revocatur." *Soliloquia*, I, i, 4 (PL XXXII,
    871).
45 *De vera religione*, c. x, 18 (PL XXXIV, 130).
46 *De Genesi ad litteram*, IV, iii, 7 (PL XXXIV, 299).

these three principles (and it must contain them because otherwise it would cease to be), it *is*. Whatever *is* is at the same time good.

Thus we come to what is probably the most often recurring question in Christian thought. If everything that *is* is *good*, what is evil and where does it come from? "Evil is that which defects from essence and tends toward non-existence" (*Idipsum ergo malum est, si praeter pertinaciam velitis adtendere, deficere ab essentia et ad id tendere ut non sit*)[47]; "I did not find it [*iniquitas*; wickedness] a substance, but perversion of the will which is twisted away from the highest substance, from Thee . . ." (*non inveni substantiam, sed summa substantia, te Deo, detoratae in infima voluntatis pervesitatem proicientis intima sua tumescentis foras*).[48]

From the fact that only God is *essentia*, it follows that what was created *is not* and cannot be called *essentia*. On the other hand creation cannot be said *not to be*. What, then, is man, if he is neither being (God) nor pure nothing? In the *Confessions*, St. Augustine calls man a *certain nothing* (*nihil aliquid*), *an is is-not* (*est non est*).[49] Man is neither Being nor a non-being (nothingness): man is stranded between *nothingness* (whence it came) and *Being* (which called him into existence/being). The famous sentence from the *Civitate Dei* reads: "Man is a greater miracle than any miracle effected by man's agency" (*Nam et omni miraculo, quod fit per hominem, majus miraculum est homo*).[50] Despite his numerous and valiant attempts, the great saint never really answered the question of what man is; and the reason for his failure is that he never found the answer to the question of how the human soul and body are connected.[51]

Because of his incorporeal soul, which belongs to another world, man is never properly at home as long as he is in the body.

---

47 *De Moribus Ecclesiae Catholicae et Manichaeorum*, II, 1 et 2. For a detailed discussion of evil in St. Augustin see R. Jolivet, "Le Problème du mal chez saint Augustin," *Archives de Philosophie*, vol. VII (No. 2), 1929, pp. 1–101.

48 *Confessions*, VI, xvi.

49 *Confessions*, XII, viii, 8 (PL XXXII, 829).

50 *De Civitate Dei*, X, 12 (PL XLI, 291).

51 *De Civitate Dei*, XXI, 10 (PL XLI, 752).

The soul's journey to his Creator is, as Etienne Gilson aptly remarked, at once a metaphysics, an epistemology, a psychology, a moral philosophy, and a mysticism. This journey begins for St. Augustine with the evaluation of human cognitive faculties. There are the external senses (which are lowest on the ladder), internal senses, and reason that is on the top of this cognitive hierarchy. Parallel to them are the objects of man's cognition. Now, since what is changing cannot be said to be, the proper object of knowledge (*scientia*) must be that which is immutable. Because only God is immutable, He is the Truth since true can be only that which is always the same (*Ecce tibi est ipsa veritas: amplectere illam si potes, et fruere illa, et declatare in Domino, et dabit tibi petitiones cordis tui*).[52] Man who wants to know the truth should, therefore, focus on what is immutable. With the knowledge of what is immutable (a knowledge gained by reason), the soul begins her ascent to God. One can already in this life have a foretaste of what it truly means *to be*, provided that one fixes one's gaze on the *Supreme Essence*. As has been pointed out many times, the famous *cogito* already appears in St. Augustine. Like Descartes, St. Augustine needs the *cogito* to demonstrate the groundlessness of the Skeptics' claim that we cannot have any certainty. However, the context in which it appears in St. Augustine is different from that in Descartes. Both in *De Trinitate* and in *De Civitate Dei*, St. Augustine discusses it as part of his considerations concerning the Holy Trinity and happiness. For a modern reader, who knows the *cogito* from Descartes's *Meditations* and is used to dry Cartesian epistemological language, the Augustinian *cogito* must seem somewhat strange. One would like to ask: what does the Holy Trinity and happiness have to do with the *cogito* or *being*? Because everything created is changing, it never really *is*. To be happy for St. Augustine is *to be*, and *to be* is to enjoy the presence of He who *Is* – that is, God in the Holy Trinity.

A man who directs his judgments in accordance with what is eternally true can already in this life have a foretaste of what it is *to be* (happy).[53] And inversely, when man turns himself from the

52 *De libero arbitrio*, II, 13, 35 (PL XXXII, 1260).

53 "Constituamus ergo anima talem sapientem, cujus anima rationalis jam sit particeps incommutabilis aeternaeque veritatis, quam de omnibus suis

eternal and immutable Truth, directing his gaze toward what is changeable and perishable,[54] he abandons higher goods for lesser ones, and thus loses himself in what only *appears* to be. In ontological terms, the consequence of this turning away from *Being* is *privation* of being, resulting in one's tending toward nothingness. In the moral realm, this turning away from God inevitably leads man astray from the path of righteousness.

V

The above is merely a very brief survey of St. Augustine's theological metaphysics, but it suffices for our present purposes. How much of it do we find in Descartes? Virtually all of it.

(1) Error in Descartes, like evil in St. Augustine, is *privation* of being or defect (*tantummodo esse defectum*;[55] *defectus substantiae . . . contra naturam*;[56] and *malum ex defectu non ex profectu*[57]).

(2) To account for error (evil), Descartes, like St. Augustine, juxtaposes uncreated *Essence* (*ens summe perfectum*) with created *essence*. Descartes remarks that insofar as man is not the highest *Being*, he *participates* in non-being. St. Augustine in turn claims that because creatures were created *ex nihilo* they by their very nature tend toward nothingness (*Tanto utique deterior, quanto ab eo quod summe est, ad id quod minus est virgit, ut ipsa etiam minus sit. Quanto autem minus est, tanto utique fit propinquior nihilo*).[58]

(3) What or who is man? In contradistinction to God, whom St. Augustine calls that "who himself is not in degree, but He is, He is"

actionibus consultat, nec aliquid omnino faciat, quod non in ea cognoverit esse faciendum, ut ei subditus eique obtemperans recte faciat." *De Trinitate*, III, iii, 8 (PL XLII, 872).

54 "Loca offerunt quod amemus, tempora surripiunt quod amamus et relinquunt in anima turbas phantasmatum, quibus in aliud atque aliud cupiditas incitetur." *De vera religione*, c. xxxv, 65 (PL XXXIV, 151).

55 AT VII, 54; CSM II, 38.

56 *Contra Epist. Manichaei*, c. 33 (PL XLII, 199).

57 *Contra Secund. Manich.*, c. 15 (PL XLII, 590).

58 *Contra Secund. Manich.*, c. 15 (PL XLII, 590). "Quapropter quamvis sit malum corruptio, et quamvis non sit a Conditore naturarum sed ex eo sit, quod de nihilo factae sunt." *Contra Epist. Manichaei*, c. 38 (PL XLII, 203).

(*qui non aliquo modo est, sed est, est*),[59] man is *nihil aliquid* (*a certain nothing*), *est non est* (*an is is-not*). "I cast mine eyes upon those other creatures beneath thee, and I perceived, that they neither have any absolute being, nor yet could they be said to have no being" (*Et inspexi cetera infra te, et vidi nec omnino esse nec omnino non esse: esse quidem, quoniam abs te sunt, non esse autem, quoniam id quod es non sunt*).[60] Descartes in turn calls man a middle something between God and nothing or Being and non-being (*medium quid inter Deum et nihil*).[61]

Furthermore, man, St. Augustine claims, is a dweller of two worlds: his soul belongs to the world changeable only in time, while his body inhabits the world which is subject to change in both space and time: "There is a . . . manner of contact of spirit with body which produces a living being; and that conjunction is utterly amazing and beyond our powers of comprehension. I am speaking of man himself" (*iste alius modus, quo corporibus adhaerent spiritus. . .*).[62] Because of his inexplicable nature, man "is a greater miracle than any miracle effected by man's agency" (*omnino mirus est, nec comprehendi ab homine potest, et hoc ipse homo est*).[63] Descartes was in equal measure unsuccessful in defining the connection between mind and body. In his private note, among the three miracles, Descartes lists free will which does not fit the structure of his deterministic universe.

(4) To explain *how* the will comes to make incorrect choices (this question should not be confused with *why* the will makes incorrect choices), St. Augustine observes that it is because "I lack the strength to fix my eye long upon them [the invisible things of Thee]: but my infirmity (*infirmitate*) being beaten back again, I returned to my wonted fancies . . ."[64] Likewise Descartes, who could also find this idea in Gibieuf,[65] ascribes it to a weakness

---

59 *Confessions*, XIII, 31.
60 *Confessions*, VII, xi.
61 AT VII, 55; CSM II, 38.
62 *De Civitate Dei*, XXI, 10 (PL XLI, 752).
63 *De Civitate Dei*, Bk. X, 12.
64 *Confessions*, VII, 17.
65 "Des deux recommandations du Philosophe [Descartes], la second seulement ressemble au conseil indirect de Gibieuf. Là où l'oratorien, trop pris

(*infirmitas*) in man which does not always allow him to "inhere fixed in one and the same cognition" (*ut non possim semper uni & eidem cognitioni defixus inhærare*).[66]

(5) Finally, according to St. Augustine, "all sins are contained in . . . turning away from things divine and truly everlasting, [and then man] is turned to things changeful and uncertain" (*omnia peccata hoc uno genere contineri, cum quisque avertitur a divinis, vereque manentibus; et ad mutabilia atque incerta convertitur*). "When the will turns away from the unchangeable and common good. . . it sins" (*voluntas autem aversa ab incommutabili et communi bono . . . peccat*).[67] Descartes provides a virtually identical explanation for error: when I am unable to fix my gaze on truth, the will becomes indifferent and it "easily turns away from the true and the good, and thus both am I deceived and do I sin" (*ad quae cum sit indifferens, facile a vero & bono defectit, atque ita & fallor & pecco*).[68]

(6) Last but not least, Descartes's theory of the unlimited scope of human will, probably the most unusual and original item in Descartes's philosophical armory, can be found in Gibieuf, who in turn borrowed it from the sixteenth-century Cardinal Contarini.

par sa controverse, constatait une carence et recommandait d'y remédier par l'effort, le philosophe préoccupé de donner des règles d'action où la considération des fins n'est pas envisagée demand à l'intelligence de ne pas se relâcher et de tenir ferme sur une vérité une fois entrevue. Pour être différente dans leur aboutissement, le cheminement des deux pensées mérite d'être signalé: il montre à l'évidence que Descartes en partant des positions du théologien mais en les querelles stériles et les considérations théoretiques, fait faire un pas considérable 'pour parvenir à la connaissance de la vérité' et donc pour que le choix moral soit plus assuré. Car, il faut bien le reconnaître, le constant rappel 'd'adhérer à Dieu' qui est le leitmotiv très bérullien du système Gibieuf manque trop souvent de contenue pratique et de règles précises. Il se trouve au contraire que Descartes qui se défend de le faire y parvient plus efficacement, car sans exacte appréhension du bien on ne peut le poursuivre. Pour faire le bien il faut sans cesse rectifier son jugement." F. Ferrier, *La pensée philosophique du Père Guillaume Gibieuf 1583–1650*, vol. II, pp. 15–16.

66   AT VII, 62; CSM II, 43.
67   *De libero arbitrio*, I, xvi, 35 (PL XXXII, 1240); cf. *ibid.*, II, xix, 53 (PL XXXII, 1269).
68   AT VII, 58; CSM II, 41. See also *Principles of Philosophy*, I. 23.

As intelligence is very ample because it understands everything, the will itself is also very ample and extends itself
towards all the kinds of good and the universal Good itself .
. . a spontaneous human will . . . unconfined by anything,
but free and with no limits, stretches itself no less to any
good as it does to the universal good.

*cumque intellectus amplissimus sit quoniam intelligit
omnia, voluntas etiam ipsa amplissima est, seseque ad
omnia bonorum genera, atque ad Bonum ipsum universum extendit intellectus . . . . Spontanea ergo voluntate
homo . . . neque ullo termino circumscripto, sed amplo, ac
libero movetur arbitrio, quod tum ad singulat um ad universum bonum extenditur.*[69]

If we did not know that the author of this passage is Contarini, we
would not hesitate to ascribe it to Descartes, who in a famous passage from the Fourth Meditation talks about the ample and perfect
will which is not limited by anything (*sola est voluntas sive arbitrii libertas . . . ut nullius majoris ideam apprehendam*).[70]

(7) Furthermore, there are several points, which are essential
both for Gibieuf and Descartes, where Gibieuf's thought and
Descartes's philosophy seem to converge. Why does man arrive at
indifference, that is, hesitation before making a decision? Gibieuf
invokes man's habit, moral weakness, and attraction to what is
easy.[71] To understand that the freedom of indifference is not an

69 The whole fragment quoted by Gibieuf (*De Libertate*, p. 44) reads: "*Cum,
inquit* [Contarini in tractatu *De libero arbitrio*], *hominis voluntas facultas quedam sit & appetendi vis quae intellectum sequitur & ad omnia
se extendit ad que ipse se extendit intellectus, cumque intellectus
amplissimus sit quoniam intelligit omnia, voluntas etiam ipsa amplissima est, seseque ad omnia bonorum genera, atque ad Bonum ipsum
universum extendit, quare praecdente cognitione in finem ut finis est
fertur; & media quae sibi accommodata fini videntur, eligit. Spontanea
ergo voluntate homo, proprio, neque ullo termino circumscripto, sed
amplo, ac libero movetur arbitrio, quod tum ad singulat um ad universum bonum extenditur.*" Gasparis Contareni Cardinalis, *OPERA*, Pariis,
Apud Sebastianum Nivellium, Sub Ciconis in via Iacobaea, 1571, *De
Libero Arbitrio* (pp. 597–603), p. 599. I have retained the original punc-
tuation from Contarini's work, which was slightly changed by Gibieuf.

70 AT VII, 57; CSM II, 40.

71 *De Libertate*, pp. 272–3 (cf. Ferrier, *ibid.*, vol. II, p. 13). There are several other points that Descartes could have borrowed from St. Augustine via

ideal of liberty, Gibieuf goes on to remark, one needs to change his habits and make an effort. In the Fourth Meditation Descartes says something very similar:

> What is more, even if I have no power to avoid error in the first way just mentioned, which requires a clear perception of everything I have to deliberate on, I can avoid error in the second way, which depends merely on my remembering to withhold judgment on any occasion when the truth of the matter is not clear. Admittedly, I am aware of a certain weakness in me, in that I am unable to keep my attention fixed on one and the same item of knowledge at all times; *but by attentive and repeated meditation I am nevertheless able to make myself remember it as often as the need arises, and thus get into the habit of avoiding error.*[72]

In other words, there where the Oratorian recommended "effort," the philosopher suggested a rule of firmly holding to the truth once we catch sight of it. Gibieuf's constant reminder to "adhere to God" (a Bérullian leitmotiv) is reminiscent of Descartes's idea of rectifying a judgment.

As we can see, despite Descartes's strenuous effort to avoid religious terminology, the core of Cartesian metaphysics clearly betrays religious, and more precisely, Augustinian provenance. All

Gibieuf. The idea of evil as privation, which Gibieuf describes as the return to nothingness: "Ex parte principii, quia non qua capax Dei operatur, sed qua ad inferiorem gradum declinans propria defectibilitate & nihilo, unde nondum omnino emersit" (*De Liberate*, p. 271); next, the idea that the perfection of creation should be looked at not from a perspective of a perfection of an individual part but from the perspective of creation as the whole: "Videlicet, etsi multa mala sint, relata ad creaturas et naturas earum, ad providentiam tamen comparata, omnia bona sunt, satem per modum medii, quia omnia ad bonum aliquod conferunt" (*De Libertate*, p. 441). Cf. St. Augustine, *Enchiridion*, chpt. 11, 95, 96, 99, 100.

72   "Ac praeterea, etiam ut non possim ab evidenti eorum omnium perceptione de quibus est deliberandum, possum tamen illo altero qui pendet ab eo tantum, quod recorder quoties de rei veritate non liquet a judicio ferendo esse abstinendum; nam, quamvis eam in me infirmitatem esse experiar, ut non possim semper mei et eidem cognitioni defixus inherare, possum tamen attentia et saepius iterator meditatione efficare ut ejusdem, quoties usus exiget, recorder, atque ita habitum quemdam non errandi acquiram." AT VII, 61–62; CSM II, 43; emphasis Z. J.

the elements that we listed above can be found in St. Augustine's well-known and widely read works: *De libero arbitrio*, the *Confessions*, and *De Civitate Dei*. Did Descartes read them? We know from Descartes's correspondence that he read the *Confessions*, *De Genesi ad Litteram libri duodecim*, and *De Civitate Dei*.[73] As for *De libero arbitrio*, there is no explicit reference in Descartes's writings to confirm this; yet verbatim reiterations in the Fourth Meditation (see 5) above)[74] leave no doubt that Descartes read it carefully.

In view of our findings, the answer to the question of which metaphysical tradition Descartes draws in the Fourth Meditation, the answer is: the Augustinian tradition, or more precisely, the "metaphysics" of St. Augustine himself.

73 See letters to Mesland, May 2, 1644 (AT IV, 119; CSMK III, 235), Conversation with Burman, 16 April, 1648 (AT V, 169; CSMK III, 349), and to Mersenne, December 1640 (AT III, 260; CSMK III, 161).

74 St. Augustine: "sed malum sit aversio ejus ab incommutabili bono, et conversio ad mutabilia bona" (*De libero arbitrio*, II, xix); "omnia peccata hoc uno genere contineri, cum quisque averitur a divinis, vereque manentibus; et ad mutabilia atque incerta convertitur" (*ibid.*, I, xvi); "sed malum sit aversio ejus [voluntas libera] ab incommutabili bono, et conversio ad mutabilia bona" (*ibid.*, II, xix). Descartes: "ad quae cum [voluntas] sit indifferens, facile a vero & bono deflectit, atque ita & fallor & pecco" (AT VII, 58; CSM II, 40–41); St. Augustine: "Et quaesivi, quid esset iniquitas, et non inveni substantiam, sed a summa substantia, te deo, detortae in infima voluntatis perversitatem proicientis intima sua, et tumescentis foras" (*Confessions*, VII, 16); Descartes: "nam, quamvis eam in me infirmitate, esse experiar, ut non possim semper uni & eidem cognitioni defixus inhaerare" (AT VII, 62; CSM II, 43).

A short remark might not be out of place. Descartes was accused of semi-Pelagianism by Protestant theologians, who suspected, not without reasons, the pupil of the Molinist Jesuits to adhere to this heresy too. This view is rather doubtful, although it is not impossible that Descartes was exposed to this doctrine. One of the theology teachers in la Flèche was Philippe Moncée who professed semi-Pelagianism. But given that Descartes's theory of the will was not completely Augustinian, it is not implausible that whatever "Pelagianism" there is in Descartes, he took from St. Augustine himself. St. Augustine's *De libero arbitrio* contains a number of points which can be considered Pelagian and which he later corrected in his *Retractiones*. Thus if Descartes read *De libero arbitrio* without *Retractiones* and St. Augustine's late works on grace and freedom (e.g., *De correptione et gratia*), he could very well have incorporated Pelagian elements into his theory of freedom without realizing it.

"God Is Not like Jupiter or Saturn": On the New Sources of the Styx Metaphor

On two occasions, in his letter of April 15, 1630, and in his *Fifth Set of Replies* of 1641, Descartes invoked the metaphor of the river Styx and Fates. It was on the same two occasions that he revealed his astonishing doctrine that eternal truths were created by God, and they depend entirely on Him. Referring to them twice in the same context can hardly be coincidental. The context in which the metaphor appears suggests that Descartes thought the content of the metaphor was the opposite of his doctrine of the eternal truths. But was it just the criticism of the ancient conception of god(s) that the metaphor is supposed to be the expression of? Considering the fact that no Christian philosopher before Descartes thought of God as the creator of mathematical verities, the metaphor was, in my opinion, intended to be Descartes's way of safely expressing his criticism of the Christian thinkers by means of pagan symbolism.

The philosophical point of the metaphor of the Styx and Fates is simple: according to the ancients, no one, not even mighty gods, have the power to change the rulings of the Styx or Fates, which is another way of saying that the sovereignty of the Greco-Roman deities is less than absolute.

If one accepts the publication of Etienne Gilson's *La liberté chez Descartes et la théologie* in 1913 as the beginning of modern Cartesian scholarship, one cannot but be astonished how far the research concerning the sources to Descartes's philosophy has progressed. Yet the question that still troubles Cartesian scholarship is the sources of this metaphor and, therefore, the precise content of what is being criticized by Descartes.

In his edition of Descartes's works, Ferdinand Alquié expressed the idea that no one had said that God is subject to the Styx or the Fates.[1] Francis Bacon's reference to this metaphor in his "On the Wisdom of the Ancients" suggests that the ancients did indeed say what Descartes makes them say, but which author or authors did Bacon, and Descartes for that matter, have in mind?

Before I turn to ancient sources, let me quote the two relevant passages from Descartes's writings:

> "The mathematical truths which you call eternal have been laid down by God and depend on Him entirely, no less than the rest of his creatures. Indeed to say that these truths are independent of God is to talk of Him as if he were Jupiter or Saturn and subject Him to the Styx and the Fates" (To Mersenne, April 15, 1630, CSMK III, 23).

> "But just as the poets suppose that the Fates were originally established by Jupiter, but that after they were established he bound himself to abide by them, so I do not think that the essences of things, and the mathematical truths which we can know concerning them, are independent of God" (*Fifth Set of Replies*, CSM II, 261).

In his *Metamorphoses*, Ovid makes several references to the river Styx, the daughter of Ocean, and the oath.

1. "For, although that was a savage enemy, their whole attack sprung from one body and one source. But no, wherever old Ocean roars around the earth, I must destroy the race of man:

---

1 Descartes, *Œuvres philosophiques* (Paris: Classiques Garnier, 1988), p. 260, n. 1. Alquié's position is untenable not only in view of the evidence I provide here, but also because the reference to the metaphor can be found in Bacon. In the English version of my *Augustinian-Cartesian Index* (South Bend, Ind.: St. Augustine's Press, 2004), p. 215, I included a passage from Francis Bacon's "On the Wisdom of the Ancients," where the English philosopher invokes this metaphor, following Ovid. As it will become clear in the course of this short chapter, beside the passages that I quote as Descartes's possible sources, Bacon makes reference to Diis, which Ovid, in a similar context, refers to in Bk. IV, 432-445, of his *Metamorphoses*.

I swear it by the infernal streams that glide beneath the earth through Stygian groves" (I, 185–89; trans. by Miller).

2. ". . . and with groans and tears and agonized mooings she seemed to voice her griefs to Jove and beg him to end her woes. Thereupon Jove threw his arms about his spouse's neck, and begged her at last to end her vengeance, saying: 'Lay aside all fear for the future; she shall never be source of grief to you again'; and he called upon the Stygian pools to witness his oath" (I, 731–37).

3. "Embracing him [Phaeton], he [the Sun] said: 'Thou art both worth to be called my son, and Clymene has told thee thy true origin. And that thou mayst not doubt my word, ask what boon thou wilt, that thou mayst receive it from my hand. And may that Stygian pool whereby gods swear, but which mine eyes have never seen, be witness to my promise" (II, 40–47).

4. "But this one thing I beg thee not to ask, which, if rightly understood, is a bane instead of blessing. A bane, my Phaeton, dost thou seek as boon. Why dost thou throw thy coaxing arms about my neck, thou foolish boy? Nay, doubt it not, it shall be given – we have sworn it by the Styx – whatever thou doest choose. But, oh, make wiser choice!" (II, 97–102).

5. "In such wise did Juno instruct the guileless daughter of Cadmus. She in her turn asked Jove for a boon, unnamed. The god replied: 'Choose what thou wilt, and thou shalt suffer no refusal. And that thou mayst be more assured, I swear it by the divinity of the seething Styx, whose godhead is the fear of all the gods'" (III, 288–91).

Virgil, another Latin author, in his *Aeneid* talks about the oath:

1. "I swear [Jove says] by the unappeasable fountainhead of the Styx, the one dread oath decreed for the gods on high" (XII, 816–18; trans. by Fagles).

And:

2. "Jove had spoken. Sealing his pledge by the Styx, his brother's stream, by the banks that curl with pitch-black rapids, whirlpools swirling dark, he nodded his assent and his nod made all of Mount Olympus quake" (IX, 122–30).

We also find several appropriate passages in Homer's *Iliad*:

1. "The water of Styx, the fearful oath-river" (II, 755; trans. by Lattimore).

2. "Come then [Hera, says to Hypnos, god of sleep]! Swear it to me on Styx ineluctable water. With one hand take hold of the prospering earth, with the other take hold of the shining salt sea, so that all the undergods who gather about Kronos may be witnesses to us" (XIV, 271–74).

3. "Now let Earth [Gaia] be my witness in this [says Hera to Zeus], and wide heaven [Uranus] above us, and the dripping water of the Styx, which oath is the biggest and most formidable oath among the blessed immortals" (XV, 35–38).

The above passages describe the gods' custom of swearing by the river Styx when they oblige themselves to keep their promises.[2] No god, including Zeus, the Father of all the Olympians, is exempt from the oath; once the oath has been made, a promise is binding and a god cannot retreat from the given word. If one can translate the language of the poets into Cartesian idiom, one could say: a god's act of will ("I promise to etc.") becomes inviolable or necessary only if it is made in the name of the Styx, which is external with respect to God's own nature. The Styx works like an imprimatur: it validates the promise (act of will) and obligates a god to remain truthful to his word at the same time. One of the reasons why the metaphor could be appealing to Descartes was the fact that it showed lack of unity of the divine nature in paganism. Were it not for the Styx a god could make a promise at one time and withdraw it at another.

One can argue, however, that the act of swearing by the Styx is merely an external sign of the promise, and, therefore, the Styx herself does not have any real power over Zeus. But as Hesiod and Homer say, the Styx makes gods fear her. None of the Roman authors explains why it is the case, but Hesiod does. In his *Theogony* Hesiod explains not only why the gods fear the Styx but how the oath originated.

"For there are three thousand long ankled daughters of

2   The above quoted authors do not exhaust the full list of those who mention the oath and with whose writings Descartes was probably familiar. See Herodotus, *Histories*, VI. 74. Pausanias, *Description of Greece* VIII. 17. 6 – 8; Seneca, *Phaedra* 942 ff. and *Troades* 390 ff.; and Apuleius, *The Golden Ass*, VI, 13.

Ocean who are widely dispersed and hold fast to the earth and the depths of the waters . . . Styx, Ocean's daughter, mingling with Pallas, bore Zelus [Rivalry] and beautiful-ankled Nike [Victory] in her house, and she gave birth to Cratos [Supremacy] and Bia [Force], eminent children. These have no house apart from Zeus nor any seat, nor any path except that on which the god leads them, but they are always seated next to deep-thundering Zeus. For this is what Styx, Ocean's eternal daughter, planned on the day when the Olympian lightener summoned all the immortal gods to high Olympus and said that, whoever of the gods would fight together with him against the Titans, him he would not strip of his privileges, but that every one would have the honor he had before among the immortal gods; and that whoever had been without honor and without privilege because of Cronus, him he would raise to honor and privileges, as is established right. So eternal Styx came first of all to Olympus with her own children, through the plans of her dear father; and Zeus honored her and gave her exceptional gifts. For he set her to be the great oath of the gods, and her sons to dwell with him for all their days" (ll. 383–402, trans. by Most).

And:

"Whenever strife and quarrel arise among the immortals and one of those who have their mansions on Olympus tells a lie, Zeus sends Iris to bring from afar in a golden jug the great oath of the gods, the much renowned water, icy, which pours down from a great, lofty crag. It flows abundantly from under the broad-pathed earth, from the holy river through the black night – a branch of Ocean, and a tenth portion has been assigned to her. For nine-fold around the earth and the broad back of the sea he whirls in silver eddies and falls into the sea, and as one portion flows forth from the crag, a great woe for the gods. For whoever of the immortals, who possesses the peak of snowy Olympus, swears a false oath after having poured a libation from her, he lies breathless for one full year; and he does not go near to ambrosia and nectar for nourishment, but lies there without breath and without voice on a covered bed, and an evil stupor shrouds him. And when he has completed this sickness for a long year, another, even worse trial follows upon this one: for nine years he is cut off from participation with the gods that always are, nor does he mingle with them in their assembly of their feasts for all of nine years; but in the tenth he mingles once again in the meetings of the immortals who have their mansions on Olympus. It is as this sort of oath that the gods have established the eternal water of Styx, primeval; and it pours out through a rugged place" (ll. 783–806).

In other words, the purpose of introducing the oath was to ensure veracity among Olympians.

The second item that Descartes lists in his writings is the Fates. The Fates are counterparts of the Greek Moirai (Moerae), the three sisters (Clotho, Lachesis, and Atropos), who spin man's life. Descartes's reference to them is not entirely accurate. No ancient author states that the Fates were "established" by Jupiter. Hesiod gives us two different accounts about their origin but neither supports Descartes's statement. First: "Night bore loathsome Doom and black Fate and Death . . . " (*Theogony*, ll. 211–12). Elsewhere he writes that the Fates are Zeus's daughters: "He [Zeus] married bright Themis, who gave birth to the Horae [Seasons], Eunomia [Lawfulness] and Dike [Justice] and blooming Eirene [Peace], who care for the works of mortal human beings, and the Destinies [Moiras], upon whom the counsellor Zeus bestowed the greatest honor, Clotho and Lachesis and Atropos, who give to mortal human beings both good and evil" (ll. 901–6).

There is a difficulty here. Hesiod, but also Homer (*Iliad*, xxii, 413; xix, 336; ix, 41–416) and Plato (*The Republic*, xx, 617c), claim that Moirae control only human destiny, that is the span of man's life. Descartes's remark about the Styx and the Fates, made in the context of the status of mathematical verities and the possibility that as his creation they are subject to His power, seems to suggest that he thought that their realm extends beyond the span of man's life. Descartes's inclusion of the Fates can be justified only if we take his word about the Fates in the general sense of ruling over a realm that is beyond divine jurisdiction.

There is one more place that includes all the names used by

Descartes – Jupiter, Cronus, and Fates or Parcae, the Greek Moirai – in one breath. In his *Fasti*, III, 793 ff. (trans. by Boyle), Ovid writes:

> "Saturnus [Cronus] was thrust from his realm by Jove. In anger he stirs the mighty Titans to arms and seeks the assistance owed by fate. There was a shocking monster born of Mother Terra [Earth/Gaia], a bull, whose back half was a serpent. Roaring Styx [as an ally of Zeus] imprisoned it, warned by the three Parcae [Moirai or the Fates], in a black grove with a triple wall. Whoever fed the bull's guts to consuming flames was destined to defeat the eternal gods. Briareus [or Aigaion, an ally of Cronus] slays it with an adamantine axe and prepares to feed the flames its innards. Jupiter commands the birds to grab them; the kite brought them to him."

If Descartes was not familiar with the *Fasti*, the Cartesian metaphor must clearly have more than one source.[3] Descartes very likely conflated the Fates, Ananke (Necessity), and the Eumenides or Eurinies. While Ananke seals the decrees of the Fates, the function of the Eumenides is the administration of justice, or punishing for the most horrible crimes, such as matricide. Their decrees, according to ancient authors, are indeed inviolable, and their appearance in tragedies show that under no circumstances matricide, for example, can be pardoned or made to be the opposite of what it is – a crime. As the Eurinies say in Aeschylus's *Eumenidies*: "At our birth this office was ratified unto us; but the Deathless Ones may not lay hand upon us, nor doth any of them share our feasts in common with us" (ll. 349–52; Trans. by Smyth). The phrasing of the passage is reminiscent of what Descartes says: the Fates were established and the gods are subject to their decrees.

When it comes to the origin of the Eurinies or Eumenidies, Hesiod tells us that when the Earth gave birth to monstrous creatures with massive limbs and fifty heads, their Father Sky hated

---

3   Emanuela Scribano pointed out to me that Edwin Curley in his *Descartes Against the Skeptics* (Cambridge: Harvard University Press, 1971), pp. 38–41, quotes Montaigne's *Apology of Raymond Sebond* as a possible modern source of Descartes's metaphor.

them and hid them beneath the Earth, not allowing them to see the light. Their outraged mother Earth encouraged her other sons to avenge their wicked father's evil deed. Cronus took courage. When the Earth

> "placed him [Cronus/Saturn] in an ambush, concealing him from sight, and put into his hands the jagged-toothed sickle and she explained the whole trick to him. And great Sky came, bringing night with him; and spreading himself out around Earth is his desire for love he lay outstretched in all directions. Then his son reached out from his ambush with his left hand, and with his right hand he grasped the monstrous sickle, long and jagged-toothed, and eagerly he reaped the genitals from his dear father and threw them behind to be borne away. But not in vain did they fall from his hand: for Earth received all the bloody drops that shot forth, and when the years had revolved she bore the mighty Erinyes . . . " (ll. 173–85).

If Hesiod was Descartes's source, he only vaguely remembered the story and confused Zeus and Cronus. But Descartes's error has no bearing on the point he makes, namely, that gods' powers stop where the Eumenides' jurisdiction begins.

Apollo's conflict with the Eumenides in Aeschylus's *Eumenides* and Euripides' *Oresteia* is a good illustration of the clash between a god and another tribunal. The god Apollo entices Orestes to kill his mother Clytemnestra, for killing her husband Agamemnon, Orestes' father. Because the act of avenging one's father is the filial obligation, Orestes has no choice but to kill his mother. The crime of matricide must be avenged. Orestes is pursued by the Eumenides, and Apollo intervenes on Orestes' behalf. What we witness here is a very clear-cut conflict between the Eumenides, who demand retribution, since matricide is evil (in itself), and a god who attempts to change their ruling. Had Apollo the power to override the Eumenides' power, the Greeks would have gained an insight into what Descartes's doctrine of the eternal truths implicitly points to: good and evil are divine decrees.

In the characteristic way of Greek tragedy, the reasons for killing and punishing are evenly distributed; the tragic conflict is in its very nature insoluble. Although Orestes is ultimately acquitted thanks to the citizenry's ballot vote, devised by the playwright, clearly, to find a partial solution to the conflict between a god and the Eumenides, Apollo's victory can in no way be considered as a triumph over them. Neither can it suggest that an Olympian is free to disregard the decision of the Eumenides who represent absoluteness of right and wrong, good and evil. However, one can make the opposite claim, the fact that the Eumenides do not get their due can imply that their power over the gods is not, as Descartes's statement implies, absolute either.

The conflict between Apollo and the Eumenides is, I believe, the only known case when the reasons of a divinity and those of another agency clash so directly.[4] Also, it is the only case that expresses Descartes's contention, without necessarily completely supporting it, that the Greek gods were not totally free of the ruling of "the Fates." The outcome of the conflict between Apollo and the Eumenides both supports and denies the philosopher's contention.

Another source of Descartes's metaphor of the Fates could be Plato. In his *Republic*, X, 617c (trans. by Shorey), Plato says: "And there were three others who sat round about at equal intervals, each one on her throne, the Fates, daughters of Necessity, clad in white vestments with filled heads, Lachesis, and Clotho, and Atropos . . ." Here, however, the Fates are the daughters of Necessity (Ananke), not Zeus, but there is no suggestion that the Fates control anything with the exception of human destiny.

The references that I provided exhaust the list of major authors[5] whom Descartes could have had in mind when he invoked

4   One can think here also of the conflict between Creon and Antigone in Sophocle's *Antigone*. We witness the clash of reasons between the king who refuses the burial of a traitor to one's country and Antigone, who must bury her brother's body to fulfill a religious obligation dictated by "eternal law." Be that as it may, although eternal law is invoked, there is no explicit or implicit suggestion on Sophocles' part that the gods are the guardians of it, and therefore the conflict between Creon and Antigone can be interpreted as a clash between god(s) and some other agency.

5   See Pausanias, *Description of Greece* VIII, 17. 6–8; Seneca, *Phaedra* 942 ff. and *Troades* 390 ff; Apuleius, *The Golden Ass*, VI, 13.See also Herodotus, *Histories*, VI. 74 (trans. by de Sélincourt). The ancient historian describes how the Spartan Cleomenes makes Arcadians swear by all

the Styx metaphor. Descartes's metaphor is not a reiteration of any of them, but rather a collage of impressions gathered from his school years reading of different authors.

The ancient sources are saturated with references to the oath by the Styx, Ananke, the Fates, and the Eumenides. None, with the exception of the more obscure writers, can or should be entirely excluded. However, the exact answer to the question of Descartes's source cannot be given without knowing with which of them Descartes was familiar. Given the predominance of Ovid in the study of Latin strongly suggests that Ovid was the primary source of Descartes's metaphor.

One last thing that remains to be answered is why did Descartes think it imperative to bring in the metaphor on two occasions in the context of the doctrine of the eternal truths? There are, in my opinion, at least two explanations.

If we look at the relationship between Descartes and other Christian philosophers, the metaphor, at least on rhetorical level, minimizes the difference between Descartes and them: it implies that the pagans, in contradistinction to the Christians, misunderstood the nature of the deities as a matter of course. In invoking it Descartes probably wanted to appear as someone who represents an "orthodox" Christian position. Given the chasm between his eternal-truths doctrine and the position assumed by other Christian thinkers with respect to the status of the eternal truths, Descartes's alleged "orthodoxy" could be measured only by the distance from the erroneous position of the pagans.

However, if one looks at the metaphor from the point of view of the eternal-truths doctrine, which removes virtually any limits on God's powers, including those imposed by Christian thinkers, it implies that any conception of God, other than that of Descartes likens God to the pagan Jupiter.

The metaphor is not a philosophical argument; it is a rhetorical devise construed and invoked for the purpose of distancing oneself from the alleged errors of the ancients. In invoking it,

sorts of things, including the Styx, leading them to Nonacris, near their city Phoenus, "for it is here at Nonacris, I should add, that the Arcadians believe the waters of the Infernal River to be visible."

Descartes most likely wanted to safely downplay the novelty of his eternal truths doctrine which the readers, most notably Leibniz, fully realized only several decades later.[6]

6   Leibniz, to my knowledge, was one of the very few philosophers (Bossuet was another) to notice that if one extends Descartes's reasoning concerning the status of the eternal truths of mathematics to moral truths, the danger of the doctrine can be clearly seen. It implies that moral precepts could be different from, or opposite to, the ones we know. God, as Leibniz says, would be like a tyrant who would have to be praised regardless of what He does. See his *Theodicy*, paragraphs 176 and 177; and *Discourse on Metaphysics*.

Subject Index